Peggy
of the Flint Hills

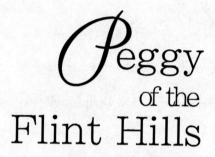

Peggy
of the
Flint Hills

a memoir

by
Zula Bennington Greene

♦

introduced by
Eric McHenry

WOODLEY PRESS

Cover and interior designed by Leah Sewell
lsewell.tumblr.com

The Woodley Press Collection
The Bob Woodley Memorial Press
Department of English
Washburn University Topeka, KS 66621
washburn.edu/reference/woodley-press/index.html

WOODLEY PRESS

ISBN 978-0-9854586-5-2

For My Family
(particularly my grandson David,
who nagged me to keep at it)

$\mathcal{C}$ontents

$\mathcal{A}$cknowledgments

Peggy would want to thank Dotty Hanger and the late Gene DeGruson first. Without them, this book would not exist. It also benefited from the wisdom and vision and guidance of Leah Sewell, Miranda Ericsson-Kendall, Thomas Fox Averill, Susan Holm, David Wexler, and James A. McHenry, Jr. It was produced with considerable help from Washburn University, including a generous grant from the Center for Kansas Studies and additional support from the Friends of Mabee Library and the Department of English. Several of its chapters first appeared in *Little Balkans Review*.

$\mathcal{I}$ntroduction

Unlike all of the other houses on the 1200 block of Mulvane Street, the one immediately north of ours faced south—the view from its large living room window was of our front porch. And I knew from an early age that its occupant, a kind old woman with owlish glasses and three feet of silvery hair gathered up in a bun, was, in fact, watching us, because if my brother or I tried to sell rainwater from that porch, or saved a butterfly from our cat, or said something endearingly insensitive, a few days later grownups would start telling us they'd read about it in the paper.

Our next-door neighbor was Zula Bennington Greene— "Peggy" to all but her oldest friends, and "Peggy of the Flint Hills" to the rest of Topeka. From 1933 until her death in 1988 she wrote six columns a week for the *Topeka Daily Capital* and its successor, the *Topeka Capital-Journal*—about 17,000 columns altogether. She wasn't a political columnist or a sports columnist or an arts columnist, but an old-fashioned general-interest columnist, full of wise observations and wry musings about whatever was happening in the world and the neighborhood. It was a job that required her to pay attention to everything from wars and elections to what the neighbor boys were up to. And it was the perfect job for Peggy, who had no grand theories or inflexible opinions but who had something interesting to say about everything.

Because she was genuinely interested in everything. A Missouri farm girl who had grown up wondering if she'd ever see a house with a doorbell, Peggy loved to seek out the novel and scrutinize the familiar, and to discover each in the other. One week's writings might include a portrait of her grandmother, a critique of the president's recent speech, a story she'd heard at a dinner party, and a eulogy for a movie star. When the Beatles came to Kansas City for the first time in 1964, Peggy accompanied her granddaughter, Melissa, to the concert: "In time the curtain parted and the Beatles were bowing as a great scream tore from young throats and bulbs flashed like heat lightning."

Peggy was easily dazzled, as the truly observant often are. She missed no nuance and made startling connections, and she was uncommonly skillful with a simile. A few weeks before the Beatles concert she had written that "the japonica and forsythia are lazy this year. The blooms come slow and scattered, like the first grains of popping corn." Nor were her descriptions merely decorative. Twenty-two years earlier, in the depths of World War II, blooming japonica had prompted a very different meditation:

> There is one pleasant association this spring with the name "Japan"—the Japan quince, or japonica, that sturdy pioneer shrub with its rose-red blossoms peeping out from the green leaves like shy children. The Japanese people have a deep love for flowers and are famous for their arrangement. Perhaps the sight of a blossom on the stem is gladdening their hearts this April, for their sons and husbands too are at war and they too suffer grief and deprivation.

This was not an easy or an idle empathy. Her own son, Willard, was serving overseas at the time, and fellow feeling for the Japanese people must have been at a historic low in Middle America. Yet Peggy could look into her own garden and see their troubled faces. "A pair of eyes like Peggy has is worth far more than a college education or a trip around the world," her friend William Allen White wrote. "She can get more out of life staying at home than most people can traveling."

Needless to say, as a child I had no idea that Peggy was a brilliant prose stylist. What was that? I knew only that she was the grandmotherly neighbor who took care of my brother and me when we were sick and our parents were working, and who invited us over to watch TV movies and Royals games and, at 3 in the morning, the Royal Wedding, and who made us pancakes in the shapes of our initials, and who shared our love of cats, and whose laugh made me want to laugh, and who seemed just a little more celebratory than most of the grandmotherly types I knew. (When my mother turned 40 and joked about feeling old, I reminded her that Peggy had turned 40 in 1935.) And of course I knew that she was well-known—an important person who from time to time would lend a little of her celebrity to my family. But I hadn't given much thought to why she was important.

It wasn't until the slow afternoons of my late adolescence that I began to pick up *Skimming the Cream*, a book of her selected columns, from our coffee table, and to consider its author as an author. Having a short attention span, I started with the shorter excerpts, which were invariably funny, but in an understated way that challenged my unsubtle brain: "A new use has been found for the manure spreader, which stands idle much of the time. Two different aspirants to public office have plastered their posters on one such machine standing near the highway."

Eventually I graduated to the longer columns, lingering over the ones that recorded Peggy's reactions to historic events: the Dust Bowl, the rise of Hitler, the assassinations of the Kennedys, the resignation of Nixon, the bicentennial, Three Mile Island. I read "Great Soul," her elegy for Gandhi, so many times that I committed passages to memory: "Gone to join the select company of the great is the little dark-skinned man whose ashes are being borne out to sea by the old sorrowing waters of the Ganges." And I marveled at her column of June 13, 1966, for which she had strolled the streets in the eerie aftermath of the great tornado: "A bath towel was driven into a door at the Embassy apartments so firmly that a man could not pull it out." At a time when most of Topeka was preoccupied with the loss of property, Peggy foresaw that another loss would shape the city even more indelibly:

> It was a tragic destruction of trees in the scorching sweep across the city. Estimates have been made of the number of homes and businesses destroyed, but

there is no way to count the death of the trees.
If money is available, houses can rise quickly again,
but the trees cannot be replaced in a generation.

In the final paragraphs Peggy exchanged her point of view for a child's, concluding the column with the gentlest of gestures:

Children played on fallen trees, making believe they were bridges. A small girl on West 17th spoke to me, "You know what I got from the tornado?" I asked what it was. "A piece of tree," she said brightly. "I'll run and get it." She proudly brought a little chip, fresh from inside a tree, as her cherished souvenir.

In a deracinated city, this was the necessary voice of rootedness—steady, alert, tender, the tiniest bit ironic, but mindful too of the beauty and wonder that can be salvaged even from devastation. Reading these columns, I came to understand why so many Topekans would stop what they were doing once a day and listen to Peggy. She said things no one else in town would think to say—or, in any case, to say so well. She wasn't just my family's loving and level-headed friend, she was everyone's.

Even so, I wasn't sure what to expect when her daughter, Dotty Hanger, asked me to read an unpublished memoir of Peggy's early years and to help prepare it for print. I didn't think of Peggy as a book author. Granted, she had produced the equivalent of *War and Peace* twenty times over, but her métier was the column. Would her sketch-artist's style work on such a broad canvas?

I was unprepared, in other words, for the small masterpiece that follows this introduction. In the summer of 2009 I sat down with the manuscript and my red grading pen, which I ended up using mainly to put exclamation points in the margins. Peggy had a preternatural memory, and could call back every hue and texture of her childhood in the Ozark foothills and her young adulthood in the Kansas Flint Hills. Here was 19th-century life—for, truly, life on a Missouri farm in 1905 was 19th-century life—recollected in rich detail and a thoroughly modern voice:

> The Hopewell church held its baptizings at another spot in Hogle's Creek. Spectators rattled down to the water in wagons and buggies, in hacks and on horseback, tied the horses to trees, and assembled on the bank. The song was always "Shall We Gather at the River," sung in voices that quavered and were lost in the distance of the outdoors. In a shirt and an old pair of pants with suspenders, the preacher waded out, leading the candidates in a line, hand in hand. The women wore several petticoats to save themselves the embarrassment of clinging skirts and they kept pushing down the skirts that floated up. The preacher took hold of a person's hands, folded them over his chest, lowered him into the water, and brought him back up again. When all had been baptized they waded out dripping. Members were generally admitted into the church during the summer, but there was always someone who bragged that they had to break the ice to baptize him. After a baptizing I always went home and baptized my rag dolls, forgetting in the excitement my distress at the length of time it took for them to dry.

"People who live in a Golden Age," Randall Jarrell wrote, "usually go around complaining how yellow everything looks." Peggy was the opposite—a woman who lived through the Depression and the Dust Bowl, two World Wars, and several lifetimes' worth of personal tragedy, yet who could always see the world's gold gleaming through. She simply loved life, and the source of that love was an astonishing ability to recognize blessings where the rest of us would see deprivations. "People who have dining rooms do not know the sensuous pleasure of eating in the room where the food is cooked," she wrote. Losing a year of school because of the whooping cough gave her the rare privilege of observing the daily routines of her parents. Losing her home to a fire was, ultimately, a merciful simplifying of material existence. Even losing a child—which she did twice—was in its way liberating, because after a year of wanting only to die she wasn't afraid of anything anymore.

I find it difficult to believe that Peggy is gone, even though I was only 16 when she died and it's been a quarter-century. I still walk down Mulvane Street and think of her, still hear her voice and her laugh, especially her laugh, still wonder what she would have said about this or that. I sorely wish I could have heard, or read, her thoughts on the election of a black president, or the struggles of her beloved central Topeka neighborhood, or the internet. I'd have given anything to be in the room when Peggy learned that she could now look up the ending to "The Laurel Bush," a sentimental love story she had read as a girl while covering the walls of her farmhouse kitchen with the newspaper in which it was serialized. When her mother pasted the final installment to the wall story-side-down, Peggy "stood wretchedly looking at it, as though the intensity of my desire might burst through the paper and make the words visible." Now someone has transcribed the whole fusty old tale and posted it on a web site—I got curious on Peggy's behalf and looked it up. I'm sure she would've been tickled to know that it was out there, waiting for her, the solution to a lifelong mystery. But I also suspect she might have declined to look—believing, as she did, that unfulfilled desire was one of life's richest gifts. I've never known another person like Peggy, and I know of no other book like this one.

Zula Bennington Greene with Eric McHenry as a child in Topeka.

Eric McHenry
Topeka, Kansas
July 15, 2011

Foreword

From the Middle of an Hourglass

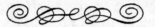

*A*ll that anyone has is his own brief span. He hugs it to him, holds on to it, and in time must let it go. Outwardly that life may be eventful or quiet, but however it is lived it is the all and now. Like the middle of an hourglass with sands running through, it converges for just a moment. In that moment the lives of parents, grandparents, great-grandparents extend from a wedge into the dim mists of time's beginning, flowing forward with children and grandchildren into the mystery of time's ending.

People wish to set down what they saw and heard and felt and did and thought. Perhaps that wish is another way of reaching out for immortality—a plea to read this, hear this, see this—our little time in the sun.

That is what this book is—something of the life lived by one woman.

Zula Bennington Greene

Part I.

Hickory County, Missouri, 1895-1910

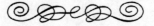

Chapter 1: This Was Our Farm

*L*ooking back, I see my childhood as a long chain of golden days. Time was a commodity that would never run out. I see myself walking slowly about the yard on a quiet summer day, an ear of corn in hand, shelling it and dropping grains as I walk. In my wake a flock of chickens—black, white, red, and "dominicker"—gobble up the corn and sing an easy daytime song of happy hens. It was not the excited cackle which announces daily duty done, but quiet singsongs that say the weather is fine, the corn is delicious, and life is good.

On our farm in Hickory County, Missouri, where the Ozark Mountains begin to make peace with the prairies, my life was not projected ahead much farther than that of the hens. Parents, food, clothes, and home were assumed as something everybody had. We knew nothing of the great world outside our circle. I, my sister Julia, and my brother George had our own smaller world within that circle.

"What can we do now?" was a question never asked. There was no end of things to do in the yard and barn lot, the woods and fields or pastures. There were wild flowers to be gathered, playhouses to be built, streams to be waded, nuts to be hunted and picked. We lived in a five-room house that like all others in the neighborhood had been built by home carpenters of native lumber and never painted. To our original story and a half (two rooms up, two down) had been added a room in which we cooked and ate. The table we called an "eating table"—no one had a dining room—to distinguish it from the "stand table," which held a lamp, books, and papers in the "big room" (the adjective being merely comparative), which contained the heating stove, sewing machine, rocking chair, and our parents' bed.

The house had weathered to the color of a summer's day just before dawn and to the furrowed texture of a relief map. It stood in a crescent of great mulberry trees. Apple and peach trees, privy bushes, and sumac dotted our yard which was surrounded by a zigzag rail fence that also enclosed a chicken yard—not to shut the chickens in, but supposedly to keep out hogs, cattle, and horses. We lived amicably with the chickens—except when the mulberries were ripe, for they liked mulberries, too. Our knowledge of luxuries being scant, we did little coveting. But we did long for a huge clean sheet to spread under the trees and passionately yearned that the chickens be banished for the duration of the mulberry season.

North of our house was a narrow road and beyond it were woods—oak, hickory, and walnut—sloping down to a small stream. East of our yard was the barn lot, with a log barn and corn crib connected by what would now be called a breezeway. (It had no name for us.) In it stood the buggy in which "pretend trips" were taken. We would snap the side curtains on and off as we imagined sudden showers. The whip standing in the buggy's socket we swished at an imaginary horse, which we slapped with imaginary reins and urged to greater imaginary speeds.

Unlike Rome, our barn was built in practically a day by neighbors, a free exchange of labor with no books kept. Women and children came to the barn raising as well, making the occasion a holiday. My mother flew about for a week getting ready. She went over the house, washed and ironed tablecloths, baked bread and pies and cakes, killed and dressed the chickens, brought the biggest ham from the smokehouse to boil. My father brought the mowing machine into the yard to cut the grass and weeds.

At a barn raising everybody was at his best, men doing something for a neighbor, men who owned their own farms and whose buildings had been put up with the help of neighbors. As each log went into place, they met and solved problems with ropes, prypoles, and pulleys. Women sauntered out to watch, admire, or squeal a warning. Their presence heightened an easy nonchalance among the men which implied that a "barn raisin' is nothin' much."

"Watch out there, Chris! Oh—I thought fer a minute a log was gonna roll down on ya."

"Wasn't nowhere near it. Th' rope was holdin' ."

The kitchen table, moved out onto the porch, had been lengthened with boards and sawhorses and spread with ham, fried chicken, mashed potatoes, beans, cabbage slaw, pickled beets, sliced cucumbers, cakes, and pies—custard, apple, peach, and blackberry. The fruit pies were stacked three or four to a plate and everyone laughed when a man said, "Pass the stack pies, please." Biscuits and light bread had been made, cornbread being too ordinary for such an occasion. Serving bowls were replenished from pots kept warm on kettles bubbling on the stove top.

My task was to stand beside the table to fan away flies with a leafy peach limb. A stye on my eye brought good-natured remarks. I was pleased by the attention, but felt my face getting as red as my eye.

The affable mood of the morning expanded. Men who wouldn't let themselves be outdone at lifting also refused to be outclassed in an exchange of wits. In that rich soil of comradery the feeblest joke took root and flourished.

"There goes another piece of pie! How many's that make, Jess?"

"*I* was working this morning." Jess bore down heavily on the pronoun.

Dinner over, the men sat in the shade of the house, leaning against the wall or the well curb. They passed around plugs of tobacco. While few smoked, almost everyone chewed. "Have a chaw" was the polite way to offer tobacco.

"Well," someone said, in the manner of the dean of newsmen concluding a press conference, "we'd better get back to work if Jake's gonna git his barn."

In the afternoon the women took lemonade to the men, along with any cake or pie left over from dinner. It had been a long, hard day. The logs were in place and the rafters up. My father would put on the clapboard roof and lay the hayloft floor. His thanks were brushed aside as the men gathered up their tools and left in the flow of a new barn and old friends.

After supper we played in the new barn. "Now you kids be careful," my father called; "don't step on a nail."

Next to the barn lot was the pasture, across which flowed a little brook that wildly overran its banks after a heavy rain but subsided into a few shallow pools during a dry spell. Minnows darted about in the largest, the only pool that never went dry. Persimmons grew in the pasture, clustering clannily together like state delegates at a convention. Over the years we ate bushels of that fruit, not always waiting for the first frost to wrinkle the skins and take away the bitterness.

Nothing is more entrancing than a persimmon tree filled with tawny rose fruit, seen against a deep bluing-blue sky.

Cedars grew plentifully farther south in our Ozark hills, but seldom on our prairies. A lone, scraggly cedar grew far back in the pasture, as conspicuous as a woman who gets into the pool hall while looking for the rummage sale. There it had to stand all its days and never knew the companionship of its own kind.

South of the pasture was our meadow, a road cutting it diagonally to the back forty where corn was planted. Timothy hay in the meadow was harvested two or three times a year—cut with a horse-drawn mowing machine, raked into windrows, then gathered into small shocks. Later the shocks were dragged to a central place and stacked for winter feed.

Dragging hay was work for a child who could manage a horse. The child rode the horse and pulled the shock with a loop of grapevine attached to minimal harness. Skill was involved in placing the vine around the shock, so that was done by a man who stayed in the field for only that purpose. If not placed just right, it could either slip under the shock or over it.

My ambition was to drag hay. Julia was a good hay-dragger. She was older and no reproach to me. But it vexed me that George, two years younger than I, was allowed to drag hay while I was assigned the job of bringing water to the field. One summer I had my chance. My father lifted me to the back of our faithful old Fred and told me to keep his head up.

But Fred was aware of my incompetence.

He began nibbling grass and paid no attention to my pull on the reins.

"Keep his head up, Hon," my father instructed.

A stiffer pull brought no results. "I think he's hungry."

A smart whack on the rump started Fred out toward the field, but after a few attempts it was obvious that I was no hay-dragger, so I was hauled off the horse and returned to carrying water. I sat on the rail fence and comforted myself with the sweet, tart, black wild cherries that grew along the edges of the meadow.

A failure as a hay-dragger, I was allowed to make a small contribution to the sickle sharpening, a task done at noon on a grindstone that stood under the mulberry tree west of the house. A neighbor helping with the haying turned it. Papa held the long sickle with its triangular blades as I poured water to keep the grindstone clean. The distance up the sickle and back seemed endless as the first section was fitted across the wheel, but I was soon lost in the impact of steel against stone, neither yielding, each forced to give something of itself, the sharpness tested against a calloused thumb. "Now don't touch that, Hon," Papa would say as he leaned the sharpened sickle against the mulberry tree to go in to eat dinner.

Beyond other fields and an old orchard was the back pasture. It curved around the west side of our farm to join another pasture next to the house, which had a pond with red clay banks. We were allowed to wade the small stream but not to play at the pond. My father was afraid we might fall in and be drowned.

This was our farm of two hundred and forty acres.

Surrounding it were similar farms of neighbors with small fields, hilly pastures, little brooks, and gray weathered houses of log and clapboard. We had no feeling of being rich or poor, only of being people in the small world we knew.

Of the vast universe I had not the faintest knowledge and, like ancient man, supposed that the sun and moon and stars were set in the sky to serve and ornament the earth. I knew the world was round and visualized it as a huge globe, half filled with earth and half with air. The sky, which clearly dropped down all around, was the upper half and the land where people lived was the middle, above the filled-in earth. This theory met all the specifications I knew and all those that were visible.

Questions tumbled about in my mind. Where did people come from? How did they get started? How was the world made? When would it end? What was above the sky?

These questions charmed and puzzled me. I still have not found answers, but am waiting for my grandson David to shed light on these mysteries. When, as a child, he asked similar questions and I had to keep telling him I did not know, he seemed to be thinking that for all the years I had lived I had not learned much. But all he ever said was, "When I grow up, I am going to find out."

Like an old melody is the memory of summer evenings when Julia, George, and I played barefooted in the yard at early dusk chasing lightning bugs. The day's work done and supper eaten, Papa sat on the edge of the porch playing a French harp, his back against the adjoining wall. With one hand cupped over his harmonica, he made "The Irish Washerwoman" and "Down on the Wabash" tinkle sweetly through the warm air.

After she washed the dishes and took care of the milk, Mamma came out and joined him on the porch steps. She pushed a wisp of hair from her face and, taking out one of her hairpins, caught it in the shining brown coil on top of her head. She was as calm as the evening star, her full skirt around her feet. There was no telephone to call anybody indoors, no television with a favorite program coming on, and we had never heard of clubs or committee meetings, motion pictures, or theaters. Parents sat in the summer dusk watching children catch fireflies. It was a small and wonderful world of glowing insects and music and slow-coming dark, so full of contentment it needed no praising.

Presently the stars would shine out and challenge the fireflies, and after a while it would be time to wash our feet and go to bed.

Chapter 2: Grandpa

My father was restless. An air of melancholy hovered about him, sometimes a quiet wistfulness, sometimes a remote detachment. He was lean, and in summer so deeply tanned that his intensely blue eyes looked like a pair of turquoises set in terra cotta. His straw hat left a line across his forehead that marked the end of the tan. His high cheekbones were emphasized by hollows beneath them.

My father liked to read, interested in anything that went on anywhere. He sat in his rocking chair, a large, plain, "store-boughten," comfortable chair padded with homemade cushions. He wore blue chambray work shirts which my mother made and trousers, several sizes too large, held up by suspenders. For Sunday he wore a light-colored shirt without a collar—the collar supposedly to be attached with collar buttons, but he hated celluloid collars, the wash and wear of that period, and ties. He didn't like mass-produced underwear, and so my mother made long drawers and a cotton undershirt that buttoned partway down with long sleeves. These were for summer. For winter the same design was made in red flannel.

We sat by the heating stove, Papa reading and Mamma knitting, children doing homework or playing. I often stood and combed Papa's hair. I liked to comb hair and if I had grown up at a different time I might have been a hairdresser instead of a newspaper columnist. Papa liked to have me comb his hair, but Mamma couldn't stand for me to touch hers; she said she was "tender-headed." Presently Papa would glance at the clock standing on the wall shelf on the other side of the stove and say it was time to be getting ready to go to bed.

He was born in Indiana, the son of Reuben and Julia Anders Bennington. My grandfather's first wife and all but one of their five children had died of tuberculosis. Julia was his second wife. Of this marriage were born three boys: John, Jacob (my father), and Frank. Two older children had died. Various causes were assigned—summer complaint, bilious fever, or they "just died." In later years my Uncle John said it was hard to get a child to ten years. About every week a little casket would be hauled through the muddy White River bottom to Tolbert's Chapel. If the mud was deep, men on horseback would ride beside the wagon used as a hearse and help pull it with ropes. This may be what my father was seeing when he seemed so distant and remote.

The boys were about eight to twelve when they learned their mother had tuberculosis. Reuben had heard that the new state of Kansas was an invigorating place for the ill, so the family set out in a covered wagon with hopes of health and a new home. They traveled thirty-one days with numerous stops in order that Julia could rest. One halt in the trip was to see an old friend who had moved to Missouri, and there they met George and Christina Holley, a circumstance that was to set my inheritance.

The Bennington boys played with the Holley children, Margaret and Laura and several younger ones. The Benningtons also met Martha Bird, Christina's spinster sister. You will hear more of her later.

Reuben took his family to Kansas and acquired land in Cherokee County. The climate which the land agent had advertised as salubrious did not heal Julia's lungs, however. One day the boys came home from school and found their mother lying on the bed, their father sitting in a chair beside her. Taking the boys aside he told them, "The doctor says your Ma's not going to get well and she wants us to take her home. We'll start back to Indiana as soon as we can get ready."

Many years later a receipt turned up in an old letter. Dated February 10, 1880, it read: "Rec'd of Reuben Bennington Eighteen dollars in full for burial and care and box for Julia A Bennington deceased."

Reuben returned to Kansas with the boys, who grew up there and went to a teachers' institute in Fort Scott. I think it was the place my father loved most. He spoke of Columbus and Hallowell and Fort Scott with the tenderness a man holds for his first love. Something he kept from those years was a square brocaded silk scarf of pale turquoise given him by a girl, I think a distant cousin. Almost ninety years later my mother gave it to me and I wore it threadbare.

An old Indiana friend who had moved to Missouri wrote Reuben about a nice single woman there whom he would do well to get acquainted with, urging that he come see her. She was Martha Bird, the sister of Christina Holley, whom they had met on their way to Kansas. Her mother had died and left a large family of children, and, when her father brought home a stepmother with a brood of her own, things did not go well in the mixed household. Martha and an older brother rented a farm and made a home for their younger brothers and sisters. In time they all married and Martha was left alone.

A widower of fifty with matrimony on his mind courts fast. Reuben's sons, now grown young men, journeyed to Missouri for the wedding and lingered on when they saw what pretty young women the little Holley girls had become. A photograph of my father at that time shows him standing beside a shock of wheat in a studio in a fur hat that might have come off a Coldstream Guard, a young man with a serious face, high cheekbones, and questioning eyes. A picture of my mother at about the same time shows her with hair smoothed from a center part, round gold earrings—she had her ears pierced—and a piece of white lace at the neck of a wool and velvet basque, a young woman composed and unsmiling. Nobody smiled while a picture was taken.

The wedding of John and Laura occurred soon afterwards and that of Jacob and Margaret a few months later. The two couples started their married lives together in the same house, the house in which I was born and grew up. (My parents bought the land after John and Laura went to Oklahoma when "the Strip" was opened.) Reuben and Martha had a house near us on the same farm. We called them Grandpa and Aunt Martha. She was our great-aunt.

When I was four or five I would walk down to their house along the narrow, clayey road between the woods and the rail fence that enclosed the pasture. (Papa didn't want me to walk through the pasture. I might fall into the pond.) "Grandpappy"—the name he called himself to us—would be sitting in a hickory rocker made by Hugh Harper. It was not a comfortable chair. The slatted back rose at a right angle to the seat of rough, woven hickory bark. (Few had comfortable chairs then. The aged sat out their last years in hard rockers, with at best a pad of cloth between bones and wood.) Grandfather would take me on his lap and doze off, his long beard rising and falling with each breath. I looked into the fireplace, saw the flame attack the wood, charge, surround, and devour it until it surrendered and fell in burning coals. I would rather have been frolicking in the garden with Aunt Martha or combing her hair, but I was afraid that if I moved I would awaken him.

Aunt Martha was a short, mousey, plumpish woman. She wore steel-rim glasses and calico dresses tied in with a long apron, although she really had no waistline. She would sit in a straight chair on the opposite side of the fireplace and let me comb her long, brass-colored hair, which she wore pulled back from a center part and knotted in the back. She had never learned to read, which may explain why she was so quiet and serene.

Life in their three-room house centered around the fireplace. A Waterbury weight clock stood in the center of the low mantel. At Aunt Martha's side was a pin cushion and whatever sewing or knitting engaged her at the time. She always saved turkey wings to fan the fire and tail feathers for a duster. On Grandfather's side were two corncob pipes, one plain and one polished. After he finished smoking he would knock the ashes into the fireplace and lay the pipe away. His two canes leaned against the side of the fireplace, a Sunday cane turned out in oak and an everyday cane that had been halted on its way to becoming a stout young hickory tree.

On the bed in the bedroom was a white counterpane and square pillow shams. On one was the embroidered motto, "I slept and dreamed that life was beauty," with an outline of a sleeping woman. On the other the woman had arisen and was sweeping the floor. It said, "I woke and found that life was duty." On the floor was one of Aunt Martha's handwoven rag rugs and in a corner a bureau of dark wood with little drawers on top.

We ate in the kitchen, sitting under a large poster of *Our Martyred Presidents*, published soon after the assassination of William McKinley in 1901, commemorating also Abraham Lincoln and James A. Garfield. We sat at the round table covered with a red checkered cloth. Aunt Martha always cooked something especially good. If Grandpa had a cold he gave me a sip of his hot toddy, but not without a few clucks from Aunt Martha.

Reuben was a man of strong opinions which he defended vigorously and volubly. Although a Republican, he was for William Jennings Bryan and free silver. He liked to argue religion and to speculate on the likelihood of the Pearly Gates swinging open for heathen who had never had a chance to be saved. Other topics of concern were infant damnation, unpardonable sin, and the Second Coming.

One day after working outside he took a chill. His sons were summoned with telegrams—sent only when someone was near death—and neighbors came in to "set up all night" with him. Then one December dusk, my mother said, "Honey, Grandpappy's gone." I remember standing in the cemetery with my head against her coat watching the lumpy soil being shoveled into the grave and making a hollow sound on the box.

We drove homeward slowly, our breath an envelope of fog in the thin cold air, the horses fuzzy and ungraceful in their winter coats. We passed the frozen creek, a mirror of slate-gray ice, the trees on either side of the road motionless, like black-robed figures braced against a sky in which the sun had not appeared that day. The only sound was the creak of our wagon wheels, a melancholy accompaniment to unfamiliar thoughts, which I found stark, hard and uncompromising.

Chapter 3: Aunt Martha

*A*unt Martha lived on alone in the house after the death of Grandfather Bennington. She seemed neither depressed nor frightened by widowhood.

The sister of my mother's mother, she was the most interesting of all my relatives. As a little girl I used to listen in thrilled silence to women's talk of Marthy's young lover who had ridden away in his gray uniform during the Civil War and never returned; of how she walked with him as far as she could, not saying a word; of proposals she was said to have refused. A wistful silence would fall on the worn faces of the women, weary from toil and childbearing, perhaps envious of the fidelity and courage which could refuse an offer of marriage, a thing no woman as old as Martha was getting to be would think of doing, unless they knew of another to be had. In the serenity and courage which life had given her, she seemed to remind them sharply of something they had missed, something they would never know. They watched her as she went quietly about her work. They would sigh about "Poor Marthy, alone in the world" and remind themselves of their own good fortune with husbands and homes and children.

She seemed not to grow old and she was never sick. Every day I went to her house—never once a commonplace visit. Although she slicked her pale brown hair back severely into a bun, wore a shapeless, calico wrapper, and never owned a powder puff in her life, although she could barely read and write and had never been more than twenty miles from home, she charmed everyone who came into her presence. She was glamorous in my eyes. Although she never had any offspring of her own, children loved her. We loved to walk or sit in a charmed silence with her, for she was not demonstrative. She was reserved, withdrawn, aloof.

A niece, Cora Henderson, came to live with her after Grandfather Bennington's death. I remember only two incidents about Miss Cora. She once swallowed a pin and she had a magnificent turned-up-in-front hat with a curled ostrich plume dripping over the brim. Word spread quickly that she had swallowed the pin, and neighbors came to offer opinions. Most thought a doctor ought to be consulted as soon as possible, so somebody rode to town to talk to him. His prescription, for which he made no charge, was a steady diet of mashed potatoes for several days.

Some time later she insisted on wearing that hat to Osceola, a town on the railroad about fifteen miles away. This meant rising before dawn and setting out in the wagon at daybreak. Travel, as we knew it, was slow. Aunt Martha urged Cora to wrap a fascinator around her head, but Cora vainly said she wasn't cold; as soon as the sun was up, it would be warm. She set the hat on top of her stylish pompadour, secured it with a couple of long hatpins, put on her coat, mittens, and overshoes (the latter reluctantly at Aunt Martha's insistence), and climbed into the democrat. (There were two ways to get into the spring seat of a wagon. You could step on one end of the doubletree or you could climb up over the wheel. Miss Cora climbed over the wheel.)

I was still lingering at Aunt Martha's when Miss Cora returned in the early winter dusk. She walked into the house with a little moan, her hands over her ears, her face raw and red from cold. She sat down in Grandpappy's hickory rocker, bent over, and swayed back and forth, giving out piteous little moans. Aunt Martha put more wood on the fireplace and hurried to the kitchen to fix supper. No scolding, no clucking, no head-shaking, no reproaches.

One day a strange shiny buggy drove up to Aunt Martha's house. Few vehicles passed along our little road and none without being noted and discussed. Nobody knew whose buggy it was, and tension increased each time it appeared. We soon learned that it belonged to a Mr. Wash Kirby. The next thing the neighborhood knew, he had married Aunt Martha and taken her to his home in Fairfield.

Skipping over a good many years during which my Grandmother Holley and Mr. Kirby died, we find Aunt Martha being courted a third time—by my Grandfather Holley. News of their intention to marry set up a violent reaction among his stunned children. Marrying his dead wife's sister! Highly inappropriate, if not scandalous! But they were married and lived more happily than either could have alone.

When I was a grown woman and married, I visited them. She still did the cooking and housework and looked after the chickens and turkeys as she had always done, although nearly eighty herself. She would nod at me in secret and sympathetic understanding of her husband's childish fretfulness and whisper kind, humorous things about him as we worked in the kitchen. "He's failing," she told me. "A man with nothing to do fails fast."

At a time when it was conspicuous for a woman not to have a husband and at least one child by the time she was twenty, Aunt Martha went serenely on her virginal way until she was twice that age. Her three marriages were sudden and a surprise to her closest relatives. My great-aunt by blood relation, she was married in turn to both of my grandfathers. Calmly she traveled down to the grave with her three husbands, all of whom declined gently and lingered, unwilling to leave her. She warmed the chill of the helplessness of their old age and softened the pangs of their dissolution. One day word came that she was suddenly dead, which is the way she wished to die.

All, except Mr. Kirby, lie in the little graveyard at Shiloh

Church. Grandfather Holley is buried beside Christina, his first wife of many years. Aunt Martha rests beside my Grandfather Bennington, her first husband. Her stone states that she was also the beloved wife of G.W. Holley. Relatives saw to it that a husband always got his name on his wife's tombstone, but her name never appeared on his.

Chapter 4: The Holleys

*I*f we had known the word, we would have called Grandfather Holley a patriarch. George Washington Holley was a tall, slightly stooped, rangy man whose thick sandy beard gave his face a square look. In a time of parental harshness, he managed four sons and four daughters without lifting hand or voice. His only punishment—my mother, the eldest of his eight, would say—was requiring a misbehaving child to "toe the line," an equivalent to being stood in the corner at school. Undemonstrative of his affections, he rarely took a grandchild on his lap.

On their rich creek-bottom farm, Grandfather Holley and his family provided their own living and security. They spun and wove wool from their sheep for the family's clothing, including his trousers, which his wife sewed and lined by hand since she had no sewing machine. One year my mother was kept out of school to weave linsey-woolsey for dresses. She said they mixed in the wool from a few black sheep to give the cloth a salt-and-pepper look.

Grandmother Holley, who was born Christina Bird, wove bedspreads from intricate patterns brought from Tennessee a generation before. The settlers in that part of Missouri had crossed the mountains and the Mississippi soon after the Revolutionary War and stopped when they saw hills that reminded them of home. Grandmother Holley had not learned to read or write and had no diversion that took her from her housework. During twenty years she bore ten children. Two died in childhood of typhoid, but eight grew up, married, and had children. She wore a perpetual look of anxiety—or was it one of weariness?—which seemed a kind of fretting foothill against the silent, mountainous strength of her husband.

Nobody called them senior citizens. George and Christina were called Pa and Ma by their children, and Mister and Miz Holley by the children's husbands and wives. Grandchildren called them simply Grandpa and Grandma. Outside the family, grandfather was called Judge Holley, a title then given to county commissioners; he was said to inspire respect and awe.

Both smoked corncob pipes, but none of their children ever smoked. It was not unusual for older women to enjoy a puff of tobacco, but it was done more or less privately. Grandmother Holley carried her pipe in the pocket of a long gathered apron worn over a long skirt. Matches were used frugally and one was never squandered when the fireplace was burning, the only heat in the house besides the kitchen stove. Instead, a live coal was taken from the fire and placed in the pipe, a task which she sometimes asked a grandchild to do for her.

Now and then my mother would say, "Jake, it's been a long time since I've been home," so on an early Saturday morning my father would hitch Fred and Prince to the wagon and we would set out for a visit to Grandpa and Grandma Holley. Papa and Mamma sat in front on the spring seat and Julia, George, and I on a quilt spread over hay in the wagon box. We rattled over rocky roads, passed through timber, and arrived at the Little Pomme de Terre (pronounced locally *pummel de tar*).

The first sign of the creek was a glimpse of white sycamores; then a turn brought us dramatically to the crossing. As he drove into the stream and stopped to allow the horses to drink, my father would point to the right and say, "In there it would swim a horse," and it was easy to imagine that we were being carried along by moving water down to a deep hole and doom, but the high drama of the trip was always the long, steep, curving hill that took us almost careening down into the valley of the Big Pomme de Terre.

Although our arrival was unexpected, we were met with the usual "Git out and come in." The men took the horses to the barn and the women and children went into the house. The spring seat was carried in and placed in front of the fireplace, where a pot of beans was boiling. Our arrival was a cue for other brothers and sisters who lived nearby to assemble for supper, some to spend the night. Soon the kitchen was filled with women and words and the main room with men and silence. After the men had exchanged greetings and brief news they found nothing worth saying and felt no compulsion to say it.

After supper the younger uncles and aunts would play "blindfold" with the children. Our youngest uncle, Sam, a baby when my mother married, was so near our age that we thought of him as a cousin. It is difficult to depict the delight it was to play blindfold by the smell of coal oil burning and the flickering light (children were warned to watch out for the lamp): flying shadows as players slipped to safety, squeals of excitement when one was caught, bursts of laughter when the wrong name was called.

Sometimes ghost stories were told. Children listened in shivering fascination and went to bed with visions of figures rising from their graves, of lights and groaning and swishing of the supernatural. We pulled covers over our heads, snuggled against each other, and talked in whispers.

Nobody really believed in ghosts, but everyone had grown up with superstitions. They were acknowledged to be nonsense, but why invite trouble by opening an umbrella in the house or carrying a hoe indoors? A good many planted, harvested, and weaned their young when the signs were right. Stories were told about "death lights," about a girl who saw a ball of fire the evening a neighbor died, and about a family on their way to visit a sick relative who "saw the light" as they approached and knew the end had already come. Some claimed to have seen blue lights over a new-made grave, and it was warned that if one wore new clothes to a funeral, another member of the family would die within the year. In some homes where a person died, mirrors were turned to the wall. Most women believed in prenatal marking of a child, and every birthmark or "strawberry" was soon accounted for.

Housekeepers were never upset by overnight company. A dozen to twenty often slept at my Grandfather Holley's house. To begin with, each bed, like an amoeba at reproduction time, divided into two. The featherbed was laid on the floor while the straw tick remained to do service on the bedstead. Pallets were spread for children, who could be placed sideways in lots of half a dozen or more. Immediately after supper the women began planning who would sleep where. An elderly or newly wed couple was given the parlor bedroom and privacy. The rest arranged in the most practical manner—age, sex, and size considered. Children played on the beds spread on the floor and were told to stay off those quilts with their dirty feet—or shoes if it was shoe-wearing weather. If necessary, some of the women slept on the floor, but men were always given a bedstead, even though it was equipped with only a straw tick.

Underwear doubled for sleeping, at home or while visiting, though women and girls always had nightgowns. I doubt that there was a toothbrush in the county, and none of us had ever seen a dentist. In those early years of the century most country homes did not have indoor privies, yet those needs were managed with delicacy and decorum. As to conversation, no swearing or improper words were heard, which included mention of sex or any garment not visible— at least not within the hearing of children.

A houseful of overnight company was fun, though I have sometimes been glad that I experienced it as a child and not as a housekeeper. But whenever I hear of company being taken to a motel because "we don't have a guest room," I think of Grandma Holley's spreading beds all over the house, her extra quilts and comforters kept on a broken chair behind the parlor door, covered with a sheet.

Additional relatives might arrive for Sunday dinner, making too many to sit down at the same table. Children sat at the second table, sometimes the third. First to be seated were the men, beginning with heads of family. The life of a man might not be easy, but he had standing. No man was ever asked to eat at the second table. The surest sign that a young man had reached adult status was his being seated at the first table, but a young woman waited for that honor until she was married. A newly wedded wife sat at the first table with her husband, often the only woman there. The women ate at the last table, lingering to taste and talk.

Soon after dinner, when the women had washed the dishes, company began saying it was time to be thinking of going home, and presently they went, urging each other, "Now you all must come up and see us," and meaning it. We climbed into the wagon, wound up the big hill, crossed the creek beside the deep hole, and rumbled home over the rocky roads.

Chapter 5: Work

*W*hen young, I was never an energetic worker. I made beds with a book in one hand. The *proper* way to make a bed was to remove everything down to the featherbed, turn it over, pat it smooth, and replace the covers. I saw that as a process which invited short cuts.

Mamma would go out to milk, telling me to wash the dishes. After I had dawdled at the dishpan, reciting some dramatic poem, I would be moved to action. I flew to the bedroom, draped a sheet around my shoulders, and recited "Lord Ullin's Daughter," a ballad about a Scottish chieftain eloping across a lake with the daughter of a Lord. Her father, watching from the shore, was frantic when a storm arose and lashed the boat with high waves. He called to her, in iambics, to come back and he would forgive her Highland Chief. But the frightened girl said to row on. Anyway, they must have passed the point of no return. She said she would face the raging sea, but not an angry father. The boat overturned and the lovers were drowned. I wept for them. I drowned with them. Then I remembered the dishes, drowning in boiling water on the kitchen stove.

Papa disapproved of fiction, both poetic and prose— nothing but lies, he said—and would question me about the stories I read. One of my favorites, published in a small daily paper we took, was "The Laurel Bush," about a governess and a schoolmaster in Ireland. The schoolmaster wrote the governess humbly seeking matrimony, and when he got no reply, went away, feeling she did not wish to pain him with a refusal.

The governess was hurt by his leaving so abruptly with no word of farewell. Her interpretation was that he did not wish to continue a friendship if he had no further intentions. I'm sure you've guessed that his letter got lost under the laurel bush and lay there mellowing while the governess did likewise. When she found it, still faintly legible, it was too late. Or so she thought. In time the man returned and called to see her. As he entered the room where she sat, his eyes fell on the thimble on her fingers. That was the next to the last installment—the last one I read.

You see, I had helped Mamma paper the kitchen with newspapers. Before each sheet was pasted I liked to see both sides in order to judge which should be exposed for reading. Somehow, perhaps when I was not present, the last installment of "The Laurel Bush" got pasted against the wall and I had not read it. I stood wretchedly looking at it, as though the intensity of my desire might burst through the paper and make the words visible.

Our work was fitted to the seasons. A farmer's ambitions were modest—to provide for his family, to save money for taxes and something to pay on another piece of land to add to his farm, land to leave to his children eventually. A farmer's wife hoped to "keep the table" with her garden and fruit and her meager butter-and-egg money. If a farmer wanted to brag a little on his wife, he would mention the fruit she had canned, and, if he let himself go, he might say that her hand was so small it would fit inside a Mason jar.

The government asked nothing of a farmer except an annual payment of property tax and sometimes a poll tax, which could be squared by working a few days on the county roads. Nobody told him what to plant or how much to reap. He belonged to no agricultural organizations and made no reports. His bookkeeping was simple. When my father needed to do a little figuring, he took a pencil from the long narrow pocket in the bib of his overalls (sometimes it was so short he had to work it up from the bottom), sharpened it with his pocket knife, jotted down some figures on the barn wall, and paid a worker out of his pocket. He had no bank account. Cash was kept in the bottom of Mamma's trunk. No accounting was needed of either buying or selling. About all that was written down were the dates on which colts and calves could be expected.

Children did chores of all kinds: they carried in wood and chips, brought cobs from the barn for a quick fire, stalked a turkey hen to locate her nest, helped with the chickens, weeded in the garden, and did small tasks in the house. Almost no work was done on a farm in which the children did not share to some degree.

Julia and I liked best to be sent on errands, especially to Hugh Harper's carpentry and blacksmith shop half a mile away. Hugh mended small pieces of machinery and made furniture from the oak and hickory trees around his shop. Curls of wood lay deep on the dirt floor that had a forge at one end. In our house was a round walnut table he made for my parents soon after they were married, and we inherited the hickory rocker he made for Grandfather Bennington. Nearly every family had furniture made by him, including small rockers for children.

Hugh was short, bald, and gnomish. Never married, he lived in a house at his shop with two dogs. Women sniffed at reports of his housekeeping (people said that a dog sat on each side of him at meals, eating scraps he threw on the floor). But the men opined he seemed to keep healthy.

One day when Julia and I were sent at noon, we finally got to see his house. He was eating dinner and neither of us missed the fact that there was a dog on either side of him catching the scraps. Everything in the house was of the same color, a kind of neutral gray. Feeling privileged at seeing the object of so much talk, we danced home with more than his customary gift, a piece of nice smelling, fresh cedar to put in our handkerchief drawer.

In contrast to Hugh Harper's home, ours was brightly colored. For one thing, we had a carpet. A long strip about a yard wide had been woven from cast-off clothing, then cut into shorter strips and sewed together to fit a room. The carpet was laid over straw and tacked wall-to-wall around the edges. At spring housecleaning time, the carpet was taken up and its straw replaced with fresh straw, hay, or newspapers.

"Just look at that dust!" Mamma would exclaim as the carpet was carried out and spread on the grass. It made a fine place to play. We had never heard of a Magic Carpet, but we made a magic of our own. The rug quickly became the Queen's palace, and the callers wore white slippers with toes. Soon monarch and callers were tumbling on the palace floor until the lady high chamberlain called out with authority, "Get off that carpet!"

The misery of tacking it back down! The first side went down easily enough, but the rest was pushing and pulling. Some places had to be stretched, some held in. Papa made a stretcher by driving nails into the end of a board. Everybody gave directions.

"It's got to come more this way."

"It can't—or it won't meet here."

"You're not tacking it close enough!"

"Don't pull so hard! You'll tear it."

By the time the carpet was replaced, even if muscles were tired, tempers short, fingers mashed, and fingernails broken, everyone stood back and surveyed it with pleasure. It was brightened and renewed. Although we children were allowed to steal a few jumps or rolls on the springy, squishy, fragrant fresh hay, this was one occasion when our parents' working together was not its usual fun.

An old book saved from those days said that the symbol of hope was an anchor. Even then I thought how much better a representation would be a farmer plowing his field in March. No matter how many times nature may slap him down, he lifts a trusting face to her in spring. His past crops may have been devoured by pests, blackened by rust, beaten into the ground by hail, washed down the river, but this year he knows will be different. Rain will fall gently; sun will temper itself to tender plants; insects will busy themselves elsewhere; the earth will loosen and confer its riches. Summer will be a benediction.

The year's work in the fields began with plowing for corn. Fred and Prince pulled the plow. Papa walked behind, the lines tied together and looped over one shoulder and under the opposite arm. I followed behind the plow, the fresh furrow cool and damp to my bare feet as I watched earth curve over the moldboard and crumble into the previous furrow.

After the ground was plowed and harrowed, corn was planted with a checkrow planter which laid out the field in a checkerboard pattern that could be cultivated in both directions. The planter operated on a wire strung across the field. Knots along the wire tripped an opening in the two grain-boxes on the machine and spilled out a few kernels at each click. I followed this Pied Piper of the cornfield, listening for the click and trying to catch a glimpse of the corn in that brief moment before it was covered by the ribbed wheels.

As corn grew it was weeded several times with the "walking cultivator," but it was the farmer who walked, the reins across his shoulders, leaving his hands free to guide the two shovels, one on each side of a row of corn. The right sleeve of Papa's blue chambray shirts wore out sooner than the left from the swish of sharp corn leaves under his arm as he reached across the row with his right hand.

Soon the welcome shade of the corn's leaves stunted the growth of weeds, and cultivation was no longer necessary. George and I tried to get lost in the tall corn, shutting our eyes and twirling about, but there were always the woods on one side, the house and meadow on the other to supply directions. We listened as the wind rustled through the corn and wondered if that might be the way the ocean sounded.

The peak of summer activity was wheat cutting. Wheat had been sowed in the fall and "broadcast" by hand. It grew and ripened through the summer. Then one day, Papa would break off a few heads, hull out the grains, test them for starchiness, and ask Mamma if she didn't think they were ripe. Her assent was perfunctory, for balls of twine had already been bought, canvases carried down from the hayloft, the binder greased and ready to go.

The binder was a fascinating machine to follow. We watched golden heads of grain bend under its reel and go as proudly to their death as a French queen to the guillotine. One moment a stalk was standing free, swaying in the wind; the next it was lying on the canvas, moving toward its final dissolution. Men following the binder shocked the bundles thrown off by the machine. If the weather was fair and the threshing machine not delayed, the shocks stood in the field till threshing time, when they were hauled to the machine on hayracks. If rainy weather left the wheat soggy, the bundles had to be spread to dry, then taken to a central place and stacked.

Finally, one day, the threshing machine would appear in the neighborhood. First it would be at Willie Iiames's, then at Tuck's, then at Uncle George Bird's, and from there to our place. A marvel of locomotion without horses, it would chug across the fields pulling the separator. Nothing created so much stir and excitement for us, who had never seen a circus.

Threshers meant cooking dinner for a dozen men and possibly keeping the crew overnight. Women would nervously question husbands about the machine's progress, hoping it would not finish at the neighbors' in time to move over for the night. When it did come, they prayed the work would be finished in time to move on before dark. Sometimes two women prepared supper for the same crew, one husband having replied, "You better have supper ready. I don't think they'll finish before sundown." The other husband told his wife, "You better have supper ready. They might finish in time to move over." A man took pride in having his wife "set a good table" for the threshers, and she did—once they were there. A threshing crew was said to talk about the kind of food they got. No woman wanted to have threshers bad-mouthing her cooking across the country.

The threshing crew, with steam in their blood and an appetite for adventure, has never been properly eulogized. Those paladins of the field roved from farm to farm, their clothes stiff with sweat, itchy chaff down their necks and in their eyes and noses, stoking the engine, mending the belt, keeping the steam up, and sleeping on the ground or floor or hayloft, with no chance for a bath unless a creek or pond was nearby. A crew we once had liked to spread a blanket and sleep in a crib of threshed wheat. All summer they went with the thresher, never sleeping in a real bed except the few times they went to their own homes during an unexpected rainy spell.

When the machine arrived it "took a stand," the engine a short distance from the separator, the power conveyed by a wide belt which the children were warned not to go near. The engine was downwind from the separator to prevent the likelihood of sparks igniting the wheat. The crew ran the machine and extra help was supplied by the owner of the wheat. A man hauled water from wherever it could be had— wells, springs, creeks, ponds—and it could be so muddy that the boiler had to be scrubbed out afterwards. The engine had an awful thirst; if the water was from a distance, horses were kept at a trot.

Men tossed bundles of wheat into the separator and in its innards the miracle of separating grain from straw was performed. Black smoke puffed from the engine fueled with wood. Straw spewed from a pipe and the belt was a noisy, endless, twisted ribbon. The man who owned the outfit leaned against a tree and watched—until something went wrong.

I liked to go to the field carrying a jug of water to Papa and stay until he "took out" at noon. He squinted at the sun and looked at the shadows to judge the time. (His big silver watch was never carried to the field.) He unhitched the horses, lifted me to the back of Fred, where I sat on the thick backband holding on to the hames, feeling the sweaty, heaving sides of the horse against my bare legs. We stopped at the spring and it seemed I would surely slide down his neck when Fred lowered his head to drink.

Meantime at the house, Mamma kept an eye on the clock or the sun, depending upon whether she was working indoors or out. Potatoes must be peeled and boiled, meat fried, and cornbread baked. A child must run into the garden to pull a few fresh onions and radishes, bring milk and butter from the cave. We set the table with our heavy Royal Ironstone made by Alfred and J. & G. Meakin, the inexpensive ware of our time. Plates were laid upside down to protect them from dust, a black, wood-handled knife and fork at each side, spoons in the spoonholder, which matched the Green Croesus butter dish, creamer, and sugar bowl. Meat was put on a platter crazed from years of hot grease. Filled with custard, a plain glass berry bowl, which had held in its years hundreds of gallons of fruit, was in the center of the table. If we dropped a fork while setting the table, we said a man was coming; if a knife, a woman. When Papa came in for dinner, he washed in the tin washpan on the porch by the well curb, cupping the water in his hands. He hung his straw hat on the chairpost where he sat. After giving the horses time to eat and rest, he went back to work.

Filling the straw ticks—which was done soon after threshing—was an exciting family task. A straw tick was a muslin case filled with straw and laid on the slats to make a solid base for the featherbed. After Papa hitched up the horses, we all went to the new strawstack and stuffed the tick full of fresh straw. As our parents worked, my sister and brother and I jumped on the strawstack, slid off, threw straw on each other, and put handsful into the tick. Mamma took a needle and quickly sewed the tick shut. When we got home there was more fun, for the new ticks made the beds twice as high and they had to be "smashed" down. That was kids' work.

In the heat of the summer Papa had the featherbed taken off and he and Mamma slept on the straw tick. He disliked a featherbed almost as much as he did barbed wire. Many people had geese and made their own featherbeds. Papa wouldn't have a goose on the place, saying they ruined the water for horses.

In the fall corn was cut by hand with a long cornknife and put into shocks, or it was "jerked," the ears pulled off and the stalks left standing for forage. Papa had a shucking peg that hung on a nail by the clock, a curved steel hook held to his hand by a leather strap. The shucked corn was stored in a crib for winter feeding.

No experience I know—unless it is laying down a rag carpet—so tests the *esprit de corps* of a family as taking down or putting up a heating stove. The pipe from our stove extended through a hole in the ceiling to warm the upstairs, then made a right-angled turn into a wall flue. To take it down was a two-story job that involved carrying sooty pipes down narrow stairs which veered sharply at the bottom. Children were told to stay out of the way.

Getting the stove out of the house was an experience equaled only by getting it in again. After the first nippy days made us sure that fall was not fooling, the stove was eased from its summer obscurity on the back porch, dust and cobwebs wiped away, and its luster restored with polish. Papa and a neighbor carried the stove low over two-by-fours. Women and children stood back, apologetic, sad for man's endless burden of lifting and carrying. A man has scant use for pity, but he values silence, and nothing annoys him more than being warned to watch out when he is carrying a heavy load. He will lift and carry pleasantly if allowed to do so in his own way.

The metal base had been placed on the floor and the stove was set down on it. If a leg fell off, no matter. Time enough to replace it later. The men tugged on the curved joints of pipe, which responded with a raw, grating rasp. Two trips were made outside to knock soot from the pipes. The damper was fitted in. Dust poured from the wall flue, over which a picture had been placed during the summer. The pipe leaned backwards like a strutting comedian. The men shoved the stove an inch to the side, three inches back, a shade more to the southwest. The pipe was straightened and bent obediently into the flue. Joints were pushed more firmly together, the missing leg replaced. It was ready to go. The men walked away with easy unconcern, talking about corn shucking, as though putting up a stove was not epic labor.

It was now time for the women and children to take over, sweep the floor, and start a fire. Forgotten were the harsh words we said when the stove was banished to the porch in the spring as the stove blazed with a brave roar that sent the room's little chills scurrying outside. Our old companionship returned. The room became cozy and warm. We remembered potato soup cooking on winter afternoons, remembered returning from overnight visits aching with cold and waiting for the first blaze, which somehow only emphasized the cold, then the blissful comfort as the warmth radiated into the room. The spirit of all the hours that had been lived in the circle of its warmth hovered over us.

Chapter 6: Church

*T*here were the Baptists and the Methodists. Each had a little country church and graveyard within clearings that held back the woods. It was a transient victory, for hickory, walnut, and scrub oak ringed the edge of each, patiently waiting their time. A few seasons of human abandonment and they would move in and reclaim their land.

My mother had joined the Methodist church before her marriage, but my father never belonged to any church or lodge. Nor did he enter into the many arguments about doctrines or denominations. He thought it would be good to live to see the Second Coming with his own eyes, to see the graves give up their dead and himself snatched to Glory without the pains of dissolution.

Because Hopewell, the Baptist church, was nearer to us than Shiloh, the Methodist church, we went there more often. It was within walking distance if you cut through the fields and pastures. My father hated to hitch up the horses on Sunday; they needed their rest, too, he said. So we walked to Hopewell, stopping by the Dietzes and walking on with some of them for Sunday School and church service once every month when the circuit rider came on horseback.

Brother Hawkins was a large man with bold dark eyes under heavy brows, a prominent nose, and a positive manner. He spoke with the confidence of an executive at a board meeting who has proxies in his pocket. Perhaps I remember him best because of a pulpit reprimand. Toward the end of a long sermon Jessie Harper and I, sitting near the front, fidgeted and whispered. He leaned over the pulpit, pointed a lean finger at us, and said, "Now you girls down there be a little quieter. We're having meetin."

I flushed with shame, felt all eyes upon us, and dreaded what my parents would say when we went home. Papa just grinned, "So the preacher had to get after you and Jessie." Mamma said, "I thought the sermon was a little longer than usual."

Sermons were *always* long. Spiritual sustenance had to be provided for a whole month. Brother Hawkins waved the Bible and shouted that he believed every word of it from Genesis to Revelation. To the faithful in the amen corner that was like "The Star Spangled Banner" and brought on an applause of *amens*. His sermon worked up to a climax—and the collection. Brother Hawkins could approach money from more directions than a chamber of commerce: appeals to duty, appeals to pride, hints of dire consequences and urgent need. Brother Peck, a sad-eyed Methodist circuit rider whose sandy hair seemed an extension of his face, always used his large family effectively. "A preacher's children," he would say hollowly, "get just as hungry as anybody else's." The hat was passed, mostly a perfunctory gesture on the women's side.

Women sat on one side of the church, men on the other. It may have been thought that a separation of the sexes would tend to direct the mind more closely to the sermon. When a young man brought his girl to church he sat with her on the women's side—their attendance practically an announcement of their engagement—and a newly married couple sat together for a time. When she stopped coming, it was assumed that they were expecting. A woman did not appear in public much after her pregnancy became obvious.

The preacher always went home with someone for dinner. If no invitation was issued, a few women held a discreet conference to decide who could most easily feed him.

Each summer, about the time everyone had frying chickens, the church held a basket dinner on a Sunday following the service. Men set up a long table behind the church. While the women were laying out the food, children wandered through the cemetery reading the stones, their mothers calling out, "Now be careful and don't step on the graves!"

The men squatted outside the circle of activity in that uncomfortable-looking position of one knee sharply flexed, the other at right angles. Women did not sit that way, nor children, nor men in town—nobody but men in the country. If bits of wood were at hand, they took out their pocketknives and whittled. A few would break off blades of grass and chew them, possibly in lieu of tobacco.

When it was time to eat, a silence settled round. Somebody always rushed in from the woods talking loudly and had to be shushed so that Brother Hawkins could ask the blessing. He stood and glared until everyone was quiet, then prayed in a loud and sure voice which said he was in good standing with the Power he addressed.

We went to Sunday School, learned stories from the Bible, and took home picture cards that had the Golden Text printed on them. We learned songs and sang them at home. The church and school were our only sources of entertainment, of hearing music or poetry. We had access to no books except the few in the school library. So I learned church songs and even now I can run through the second and third verses (if I don't stop to think) of songs like "When the Roll is Called Up Yonder," "What a Friend We Have in Jesus," "Showers of Blessing," "Beulah Land," and "Work for the Night Is Coming." All children signed the temperance pledge at least once a year.

The Baptists and Methodists had something of the attitude toward each other as state delegates at a national convention. All were there for the same purpose, but each planned to arrive at it in his own way. The two chief differences between the churches, as noted by the people in our community, were baptism and the taking of the sacrament. People said the Baptists baptized and the Methodists sprinkled, which was putting it simply, and that the Baptists held closed communion with only members of the church invited to take sacrament. They came forward and the bread and cup were passed, all using the same cup. The Methodists invited all professing Christians to partake.

A "professing Christian" was one who had been converted and saved, and the line was drawn close at revival meetings. Each church had one every year, and Shiloh, in addition, had a rousing camp meeting each summer. As the fervor mounted, inquiries were made of friends and relatives as to whether they had been saved, asked in much the same manner that one would inquire, years later, if a person had had his polio shots. Friends would ask each other of a mutual friend, "Has she professed?" I feel certain that nobody asked my father if he had been saved. He just wasn't the kind of person who attracted questioners.

Theology, along with politics, was always a lively topic of conversation in our rural community. Scripture was cited for deathbed repentance. Death was not so sudden as it often is now and people generally died in their beds after an illness. Opinions differed on the age of accountability. It was reasonably agreed that an infant who died would be welcomed at the Pearly Gates, as surely would a child of six or eight or ten. But anyone old enough to know right from wrong was thought to be held accountable, and therefore lost, if he died unconverted and, some held, unbaptized. Tougher to dispose of were the heathen. Some thought that those who had never had a chance to hear the Word would surely be saved. Others were doubtful. Biblical texts were quoted to support both arguments. The hottest discussions, however, were on the unpardonable sin, and talk always got around to that fascinating topic, which held awful, unfathomable mystery.

The church believed its mission was to save souls for the hereafter, more than to promote Christian conduct here on earth. That brought up another point—was a person who was once saved forever saved? A few believed so, but more thought a Christian could backslide, and revival preachers always had a special sermon for backsliders.

I remember the earnestness with which preachers discussed the probability of there being different compartments in heaven where people went according to their merit. It was their business to preach last-minute repentance. They stood dutifully at bedsides, holding out the hope of salvation to feeble souls struggling to free themselves from a wasted mass of flesh. But it did not seem right to them that a scoundrel who repented in the last ten minutes of his life should receive the same first class accommodations in heaven that they would have—they, who had ridden the circuit in all kinds of weather for forty years, who had lived on the meager fare provided by grudging parishioners, and whose only reward was the expectation of heaven.

Revival meetings were both social and religious occasions. If a sinner was saved and confessed his sins, nobody wanted to miss it. Revivals were thought of as a kind of vacation. Families brought food and bedding to the Shiloh camp meeting and remained for a week, sometimes for the duration, listening to three long sermons a day. Beds were spread on the ground in a row of shelters with three sides closed, the fourth open, facing the woods, which provided wood for outdoor cooking and privacy for toilet needs. I would walk past the open side of shelters, observing the scenes of domesticity, and wish that we could camp out.

"Couldn't we have a camp?" I asked my father.

"You wouldn't like to gaum around like that, Hon," he said. "The flies would eat us up and there's no fit place for the horses."

Other families brought a basket dinner on a Sunday and stayed for all three sermons. The time between afternoon and evening sermons was the best, with campers frying meat and potatoes and making coffee over open fires and the basket-dinner families setting out the remains of their food. Men were bringing in wood from the timber, horses were eating and stomping at flies, children were playing. Babies were sleeping on quilts spread on the ground, mothers fanning flies away and patting starch bags on the red welts of chigger bites of whimpering toddlers. Lengthening shadows turned the day into a soft dusk filled with pleasant sights and sounds and smells.

The evangelist and his family were the center of attention and to see him out of the pulpit holding a baby in his arms instead of waving them made him seem almost like anybody else instead of a thundering prophet. During a revival many women and girls felt a strong emotional attachment to the evangelist. Indeed, the power of moving people was his chief asset. A revival, like an athletic tournament, did not draw big crowds until interest had been aroused. A week of preaching was needed to stir religious fervor to a high pitch.

The tabernacle was a wide space, roofed, but not enclosed. Straw was scattered over the dirt floor and stuck to clothing when people knelt to pray. The congregation sat on rows of backless wooden benches and listened to a gospel of hell fire and the bottomless pit. (A boy once asked his father what the preacher meant by the "bottle of spit.") Every evangelist had a stock of stories about sinners saved by a hair. They were converted on the last night of the meeting and the very next day or the next week they sickened and died. Stories of sinners who died unsaved scared people to the mourners' bench. As the congregation sang—most evangelists had a wife who could lead the singing—the preacher raised his arms and exhorted, sweat running down his face and dampening his shirt under his suspenders. Palm leaf fans were waving all over the tabernacle. Women wore long skirts, starched petticoats, cotton stockings, high shoes, high collars, and long sleeves. Men wore shirts, with very few neckties, and trousers held up by suspenders. As they sang, people turned their heads to see who was "coming forward." Now and then a woman or two got "shouting happy."

The summer I was fourteen I was converted. The preacher

said all were born in sin and had to be saved by the Blood of the Lamb. Blood was always mixed liberally in sermon and song. Guilt did not lie heavily on me, but I had no trouble recalling my sins. Once I had told my mother I did not know where the wash pan was and I did know. I had seen it on the front step. I had not put it there and there was no reason for me to lie, but I did and I knew it was a sin. And once George and I reached up to an open kitchen window from outside and took a custard pie that had been set out to cool. We ate every bit of it. That weighed on my mind as an unexpiated sin, for Mamma not only did not scold us, she did not even mention a missing pie, never hinted that one was stolen, never asked leading questions, or gave us an accusing glance.

Another sin was my quick temper. I do not remember it, but I was told that when I was very young I snatched a pencil from my sister Julia and threw it into the fire. Within memory was a time when I was about to hit George with a stick, but he took himself nimbly out of range. Papa saw it and gave me a spanking. While no blood was shed, I felt that I had paid for that sin.

But my worst sin was my stubbornness and this made me more unhappy than any other of my wrongdoings. If something disturbed me near mealtime I would impulsively say I wasn't hungry when the meal was announced. Right away I would be sorry and know that I was hungry and would think of the family around the table passing food to each other and would feel alone and desolate. Yet when my dear mother would come to me with kind, gentle words, I still said I wasn't hungry. Something in me refused to give in. I wanted to. I was pained. But I would not.

I was converted and joined the church and felt truly that my sins had been forgiven. I learned to control my temper and yearned to do good.

Going to the pasture for the cows, with no creatures to hear me but cautious rabbits and curious squirrels, I preached aloud to the heathen creatures. Yet a few months later when I went to prayer meeting and knew that as one of the new converts I would be expected to testify to the joys of being saved, I sat silent and fearful. I cannot understand why all my life I can one day make a spectacle of myself and the next day be painfully reticent.

Julia and I joined the Methodist church and when she chose to be baptized by immersion, I said I would also. But on the bank of the creek I had one of my impulses. I went to the minister right in front of everybody and said I wanted to be sprinkled instead of immersed. It wasn't that I was afraid of the creek. I had remembered his saying that sprinkling was a sign of the spirit descending and that immersion was symbolic of the washing away of sins. Kneeling alone on the bank of Hogle's Creek, I received baptism by sprinkling.

The Hopewell church held its baptizings at another spot in Hogle's Creek. Spectators rattled down to the water in wagons and buggies, in hacks and on horseback, tied the horses to trees, and assembled on the bank. The song was always "Shall We Gather at the River," sung in voices that quavered and were lost in the distance of the outdoors. In a shirt and an old pair of pants with suspenders, the preacher waded out, leading the candidates in a line, hand in hand. The women wore several petticoats to save themselves the embarrassment of clinging skirts and they kept pushing down the skirts that floated up. The preacher took hold of a person's hands, folded them over his chest, lowered him into the water, and brought him back up again. When all had been baptized they waded out dripping. Members were generally admitted into the church during the summer, but there was always someone who bragged that they had to break the ice to baptize him. After a baptizing I always went home and baptized my rag dolls, forgetting in the excitement my distress at the length of time it took for them to dry.

Funerals were held in the church. No undertakers served our community. I never knew of such a person until a good many years afterwards. Death was generally managed without professional help, except for the minister. Every neighborhood had a woman who attended the sick and assisted at birth and death. In ours it was Aunt Martha Bird, the wife of my mother's uncle, George Bird. A doctor was called if an illness seemed serious.

Neighbors came and "sat up" with the sick and, when death came, washed and dressed the body. Sometimes a casket was purchased but more often Hugh Harper made one, a plain wooden box which women lined with cotton batting and covered with white muslin. Neighbors dug the grave and took the casket to church in a farm wagon. The minister spoke long and solemnly, picturing the person already in heaven, free from suffering and greeting those who had gone before. The congregation walked by for a last look, then returned to their seats and sat while the family made their farewells. There was talk of how the chief mourner "took it," and the demonstration was taken as a measurement of grief. "His wife sure took it hard" might be said in commendation. After one funeral one woman said, "I was sitting where I could see her the whole time and she never shed a tear." The coffin was lowered into the fresh clay, unsoftened by mortician's grass or florist's wreaths. People brought flowers from their own gardens if any were in bloom. Family and friends stood by until the grave was filled.

If a child died the parents were told that Jesus needed another angel and how much better it was that the little one had been spared the pain and sorrow of living. But despite the pain and sorrow and the anticipated joys of heaven, people clung to life. It might be a vale of tears, but not even the most earnest believers want to leave it.

It was a long way from the bland smoothness of the undertaker, his bland assistant, the frilled mauve casket, the hired musicians, everything done to soften the impact of death, all at a handsome price. Sometimes while sitting at a funeral, I think of Hopewell and the natural and simple burying of the dead.

Nobody in our family had died except my Grandfather Bennington, who is buried in the Shiloh cemetery. To read his name on the stone, Reuben Bennington, the last name the same as mine, brought a feeling of kinship with the others there with him. Everybody thought of the dead as being in heaven.

Heaven was somewhere up there, possibly right above the blue sky, where God, an old man with a long beard and a stern, solemn face, sat listening to prayers and deciding which to answer, saying who would be born and who would die, and punishing people who did not repent. Women blamed themselves for deaths and disasters in the family, saying they were sent by God as a punishment for their sins, and sometimes the neighbors said the same things.

Hell was a hot fire burning forever somewhere deep inside the earth. My image of the Devil, taken from the cover of a book, *The Great Controversy Between Christ and Satan*, was of a shadowy figure with fierce eyes, a three-pronged pitchfork in one hand. A great-aunt told us that the Bad Man lived in the woods and would come out to get the children who were not good. Though we roamed the woods every day, we never once saw him.

Heaven and hell seemed far away in time and space. I expected to go to heaven when I died, but that too was very far away. I could not imagine it ever happening to me. Old folks died, of course, but it was impossible to think of myself as ever being old.

Chapter 7: Senses

*T*he first years of a child's life are quickened by a hunger of the senses. On summer nights when our house was quiet with sleep, I sat on the floor in my room reading and swooned with the moon-flooded sweetness that came in through the window. I closed the book, my finger marking the place, and listened to the frogs in the pond adding their basses and cellos to the violins and violas of the cicadas. Garden-ripening fruit and new-cut hay blended their smells with the rambler rose outside my window. The night set my book to music.

Reading led me into new worlds. I read in the daytime when I should have been helping my mother and at night when I should have been asleep, a coal oil lamp on a chair by my bed and a rug rolled against the crack under the door to keep my parents from seeing the light. I wept over the plight of poor orphans and brave young men who died nobly and rejoiced when true love won out and the villain got his desserts. Most of the books to which I had access were sentimental fiction. Confusing myself with the heroines, I became the center of countless dramas. I snatched children from the feet of runaway horses, took food to helpless old ladies, nursed wounded soldiers back to health, and found the missing will. But the highest drama was falling in love with a darkly handsome young man.

Ladies fainted, but only when a man was present to catch

them. No one I knew had ever fainted, but then the people I knew had little in common with people in the books I read. When Lena Rivers, the heroine of a book by that name, was shown a daguerreotype that had been found in the room of an older man, she said, "It is I, O heaven, but how came he by it?" Then she fell fainting to the floor at Durward's feet. The picture was of her mother and the man turned out to be her long-lost father.

Against this romantic world the life of my parents seemed dull and grubbing, and I determined not to be like them when I grew up and married. Parents did not want to do anything but get up early, work all day, go to bed at dark, and keep everybody's feet dry.

And worry. Papa worried about fire and mad dogs and wind and water. If a dark cloud came up blowing a heavy wind, he was out studying the sky. If it looked bad enough, he hurried us all to the cave, where he would hold the slanting door open against any heavy debris that might shut us in. Through the partly open door we heard the wind and saw pieces of tree limbs flying past. One time we emerged to find the roof of our barn neatly picked up and set over a few notches and another time a tree was uprooted. Perhaps these experiences and others contributed to the uneasy feeling I have in closed places. For punishment my mother sometimes shut me up for what must have been only seconds in a closet under the stairs. In the blackness I would scream and beat frantically on the door. I became so frightened by closed doors that when I was upstairs playing with my dolls I would keep looking down the stairway to be sure the door was open. (George liked to tease me by closing it.)

I am not afraid of tornadoes, but I am uncomfortable in an elevator. In that moment after it stops and before the door opens, I am stricken with silent panic. I have walked up ten flights of stairs to avoid an elevator that had a habit of stalling between floors.

The word was not used by people I knew, but I had *compulsions.* I could not go to bed without giving my family of dolls three meals, moving them in and out of their chairs three times to touch imaginary food to their mouths. At one time I felt compelled each evening to touch my mother's sidesaddle, which hung on the porch outside the door. Nor could I fall asleep without first kissing my mother goodnight. If she had already gone to bed, I lingered. Sometimes I would hear my father murmur, "She wants her goodnight kiss." In a different time and place my parents might have hustled me off to a psychiatrist.

But the prevailing memory of my childhood is one of play. We roamed woods and pastures from early spring to late summer, bare-footed and free, wading creek branches and gathering flowers. We took them home, but they always seemed to lose their shine and glory on the way.

We stepped into puddles of water with delicious shivers at a dangerous undertaking, for their reflection of the sky made them seem bottomless. Across the woods north of the house ran four small waterways not important enough to have names bestowed upon them by our elders. We called them *hollows*. The first hollow crossed the road between our house and Grandfather Bennington's. When it rained its water moistened the yellow clay to coral and flowed through the woods to a branch which took it to Hogle's Creek and started it on its way to the big rivers and the sea.

In the first hollow we had a playhouse, a split-level built on the exposed roots of a tree. Flat rocks formed the floors. Other rocks, which bore a faint resemblance to beds, chairs, or tables, made the furniture. It was not a house built on sand and could withstand rain with no more damage than washing away the moist carpet and, at worst, upsetting the furniture.

As we grew older we ventured on to the second hollow, only a short distance away, then to the third. But the fourth hollow seemed remote and mysterious. There, we believed, the rocks must be bigger and smoother and whiter, the flowers more brightly colored, the water a silver cascade.

The time came when we could no longer withstand the lure of the fourth hollow. Over a gentle rise Julia and I ran to the second, over another rise to the third, and on with trembling anticipation and uneven breath to the fourth. . . . There it was: a disappointingly shallow bed filled with leaves. No water cascaded through it. No gleaming stones waited to be made into palaces. The trees were smaller and thinner and through them we could see the clearing. We did not talk on the long way back.

We often walked through woods and pastures, but one boundary line stopped us, a sweeping hedge row between our land and that of Fountain Gover, who was called *Old Fountain Gover.* I had never seen him. One reason was that he had a dog that Papa said was vicious. Another was that the Govers, an elderly couple, seldom left their home.

Mr. Gover was a legendary figure. It was told that when he was on the way to California in the Gold Rush of 1849 he was stricken with cholera and left behind to die while the rest of his party continued on. He recovered in time and joined his friends. A man who had practically been raised from the dead struck us with awe.

A time came when I visited the Govers with a granddaughter of theirs who was my age. As we opened the gate and walked into the yard, it seemed like entering a walled city, an impression heightened by a row of old lilacs which crowded along one side of the yard and a heavy growth of red honeysuckle encasing the fence on the adjoining side. A dog stood by while Mrs. Gover opened the door and led us into a room that was cool and dark. On the floor were braided rugs of dark materials. A table, chairs, and a kitchen "safe" were in the room. On one chair an old man sat bent over, looking into a fireplace in which there was no fire.

"I've just got the bread out of the oven," Mrs. Gover said, "and you girls can have a piece while it's warm." She turned two big loaves out of a pan, sliced one, buttered two pieces and spread them with blackberry jam. Then she spoke to her husband, raising her voice, "It's Trean come to see us and Zula, one of Jake's girls." He spoke to his granddaughter and asked about the family, then turned to me, "And this is Jake's girl?"

I would have liked to ask him about the cholera and if he ever found gold, but all I could say was, "Yes, sir." In those years of ripening senses, nothing was more enchanting than smells. They did not come in bottles labeled *Irresistible* or *Sonata* or *My Sin* or even *No. 5*. No bottled scents were in our house or in the stores where we traded, but bold and elemental scents rioted in kitchen and cave, in yard and garden, pastures and woods. There were mint and catnip, tomato vines and jimson weed that grew on the cave and in the barn lot, fresh hickory leaves and green walnut hulls, clover and timothy hay, and flowering orchards. Lying on the ground to smell fat pink hyacinths, I was transported into ecstasy. Stunningly sweet were the white mayapple blooms. There were roses and honeysuckle, irises (which we called *flags*), marigolds and chrysanthemums. Fresh chopped wood was a good smell and so was the faint, far-off scent of a skunk.

I stood beside my father and caught the first whiffs of apples dug from their winter burial in the ground, and beside my mother as she lifted the rock and wooden disk which weighed down the sauerkraut in a big stone jar. There were pickles and clabbered milk, the sharp tang of vinegar, and the strong smell of homemade soap. On washday the clothes had one kind of smell when they were lifted from the soapy boiler and another when they were brought in fresh from the line. But of all the smells, none could touch camphor. What chance would a sissy smell like *Irresistible* have against the racy pungency of camphor gum? It was worth being sick to be doctored with camphor.

Even toothache, mixed up with the smell of cloves, is remembered with more pleasure than pain. A small piece of cotton saturated with clove oil and pushed into or around the offending tooth was my mother's treatment. With the spice burning my mouth, I knelt in the rocking chair, laid my face against a pieced cushion, and moaned as I rocked, sucking in air to cool my mouth. Whether it was the rocking, the air, or the cloves or whether the pain had run its course, presently the hurt was gone and nothing left but the sharp taste and smell of cloves, the quiet purging by pain. Chastened, I sat thinking about where pain came from and where it went and why anything that could not be seen could hurt so bad.

Chapter 8: The Iconium Picnic

*T*he Picnic! In the adjoining corners of Hickory, Benton, and St. Clair counties, Missouri, the word *picnic* had only one meaning—the Iconium Picnic. A picnic as it is now known—taking food to a park or lake or even into the backyard—was rare; thus, the Iconium Picnic was an exciting event of the year. Far more than a community gathering, it was a kind of general assembly held on two consecutive days late in summer in a pleasant woods near the small town of Iconium. The event was looked forward to with as much anticipation as Christmas. People saw friends there they had not seen since the picnic the year before.

The laying by of corn was anxiously awaited, for farmers told their families that, if the work was finished in time, "We might go to the Iconium Picnic." The fact was that the picnic was set for a time when corn would presumably be laid by. If the summer had been rainy and work delayed, it was acceptable to say that it was "too wet to get in the fields." If any excuse was needed for going to the picnic, most everybody found one, even if it was only that "the woman made such a fuss I had to bring her."

Ordinarily men did not leave their work without good reasons, but the Iconium Picnic was reason enough. There remained one tough decision—whether to go for the first day or the second. Friends and relatives asked each other when they were going and word quickly circulated about who was going on which day. Some settled the question by going both days. Weather could be the deciding factor. No matter how dry the summer had been, rain was not welcome on Iconium Picnic days.

On the morning of the Iconium Picnic, Mamma brought the washtub up onto the porch by the well and filled it half-full of water, into which she emptied a teakettleful of hot water until it was a pleasant temperature for bathing. In turn each child was set in the tub and scrubbed, accompanied by complaints that their ears were being poked too hard. After the bath, toenails and fingernails were trimmed with scissors. (Papa cut his with his pocketknife.)

For everyday I wore my hair parted in the middle with two small side braids joining the two braids down my back tied with strings, but for the Iconium Picnic it was sometimes parted on the side. Whether the part was side or middle, my hair was rolled instead of braided and the back braids were tied with inch-wide ribbons worked in with the hair for a few turns so they would not slip off.

Julia wore her tawny gold hair in a pompadour which extended into a single braid down her back, with a wide bow either on top of her head or at the nape of her neck. We combed our hair in front of the one looking glass in the house, a small "wavy" mirror set high over the homemade comb pocket at a wide angle from the wall. My mother's shining brown hair was swept to the top of her head and coiled in a neat knot. I thought it the prettiest hair I had ever seen and wished I could comb it as I did Papa's and Aunt Martha's.

George was gotten up in the local version of Little Lord Fauntleroy with his best white waist and knee pants. Mamma wore a waist and skirt and Papa wore the pants of his Sunday suit, his good shirt, but no necktie. He never wore a necktie. His pants, always loose around his thin waist, were held up by suspenders. No man wore a coat unless it was cold enough to need one.

We all wore high shoes with black cotton stockings

held up by elastic garters. It was quite an art to cut them exactly right. If too tight they would be uncomfortable; if too loose the stockings would sag; if not a little snug, they would become too loose too soon. Droopy stockings were a common experience, and children were always stooping to pull them up.

A big basket dinner had to be packed. The horses were hitched to the wagon and an old quilt was thrown over hay in the back for the children to sit on. It was also an occasion for greasing the wagon, Papa smearing heavy axle grease on the hubs with a stick. Mamma, lifting her skirts, said sharply she didn't see why he had to wait until we got on our best clothes. Stepping in over the tongue, she warned us not to get grease on our dresses. The grease splotches on Papa's workshirts stayed on through repeated washings, getting only a bit paler each time.

Mamma and Papa got into the spring seat at the front of the wagon, children piled in behind with the basket of food, and we were off. The road to the Iconium Picnic grounds was an overture that set the mood of excitement for the day, for on it was the "sidelly hill," the name we gave to a short stretch of road that curved sharply around a hill. Its slant was so steep that it seemed the wagon must surely tip over and roll down into Hogle's Creek. But Fred and Prince kept their heads, Papa kept a tight hold on the lines, Mamma kept silent, and, like the Children of Israel at the Red Sea, we passed over in safety.

At the grounds, Papa unhitched the horses and tied them to the wagon bed, where they were free to munch on hay at pleasure. During the day they would be brought a bucket of water and a feeding of corn on the cob.

People flowed together from the isolation of their farms like little streams from diverse sources converging into a deep river of companionship. No program was needed. The chief activity of the day was conversation. Just to mingle with so much humanity was excitement enough. Spring seats were lifted from wagons and placed on the ground for the women;

the men squatted in groups. Much of the day was spent by both men and women in milling around to see who was there.

People learned who had died or married the preceding year, who had been born or was on the way to being born. Women talked about their gardens and chickens, exchanged remedies for pip and cholera, remarked that the hawks had been bad that year, that they had nearly enough rags tacked for a carpet, that their mother's rheuma*tiz* was a bit better, and did anybody have a bow tie quilt pattern or an ocean wave? They told each other how many jars of fruit they had canned and how many glasses of jelly they had made, who was teaching school that year, and how many grandchildren they had.

For the children, a wonder beyond the power of words was the merry-go-round, operated by one man and powered by one horse that plodded in a little circle inside a platform which held seats and two pairs of painted, wooden horses. As the platform turned, music tinkled.

The first thing a child wanted to do as soon as he stepped down from the wagon was ride on one of the horses of the merry-go-round. If plain, old, hoe-handle horses on which George and I galloped about the yard at home could take on flesh and blood, mane and tail, these marvelous creatures— the very shape of a horse—were Pegasuses on which we soared into the sky to the sound of music. A live horse treading his rounds seemed dull and prosaic compared to the fiery mounts we were privileged to ride. Looking back at the one-horse merry-go-round, it does not seem one-horse at all. Even in this mechanical age I call it ingenious that one man and one horse could operate it.

A barrel of water with a tin cup tied to it was provided for drinking. Lemonade was sold, dipped from a washtub in which halves of lemons floated like little boats in a pale sea. Three or four heavy glass tumblers were provided for serving. It cost a nickel a glass, the same price as a ride on the merry-go-round.

Now and then someone would bring an ice cream freezer and sell ice cream at ten cents a dish. A crowd gathered to watch it being made, a man turning the crank while a good-sized chunk of a boy sat on the freezer to hold it steady. Salt and ice were added as the freezing progressed. Ice was brought from Osceola, a town a few miles away, where it had been preserved in sawdust since it had been cut from the Osage River the winter before. Ice was the greatest of luxuries. As I watched it being scooped into the freezer I coveted a tiny piece to hold in my mouth.

We never bought ice cream. Few did. Most of that luxury trade was from young men who had brought girlfriends and were being big spenders. People watched them eat as they sat chatting at a rough wooden table, and some of us were envious.

Several families spread their dinners together on a cloth on the ground. This was the peak of the day for the women who had prepared the food. There was no county fair in which to display cooking and gardening skills, but here was an audience to see and taste and pass judgment.

Women had set hens early with an eye to having frying chickens for the Iconium Picnic. They had coaxed tomatoes and watermelons and sweet corn into maturing for this day. Nothing came out of a store. The food had been grown and cooked by the women who set it out with modest pride. They made excuses for their runny cake frosting and praised each other's pies and preserves. A jar of beet pickles was usually turned over, which occasioned talk about how to take the magenta stain out of the tablecloth.

"I'm going to save some of these seeds," a woman would say of the extra fine tomato or watermelon. Tomato seeds would be spread on a paper to dry, watermelon seeds tucked away in an empty jar or pan. "Receipts" were exchanged for dishes eaten that day and for others remembered from former picnics. Few women cooked from cookbooks. They *remembered* recipes.

"My cake from that receipt you gave me last year

was nowheres near as good as yours. Now what did I do wrong?"

That question would start a discussion of techniques in cake baking which moved on to techniques in cooking in general, to housekeeping and child rearing. Close friends confided troubles they were having with their children or relatives or neighbors.

After the food was cleared away, women took their children into the comparative privacy of the woods (no toilets were provided). Babies and young children slept on quilts spread in a shady spot, their mothers sitting beside them fanning away the flies which were having a picnic too. Older children roamed about alone, free from maternal supervision, a coveted privilege and a mark of growing up.

"Aw, please let me go around by myself this year," a child would plead. "I won't get hurt. Johnny gets to go around alone and he did last year, too," mentioning a friend about his age. If permission was granted he would tell everybody on the first day of school, "I got to go around by myself at the Iconium Picnic this year."

After dinner a ball game started as soon as two teams could be lined up. Some men preferred to pitch horseshoes or talk about crops and candidates. Quite a little business was done at the Iconium Picnic. Handbills with smudged pictures of stallions and jacks advertising stud service were tacked to trees. Some guaranteed a mare in foal; others promised the colt to stand and suck. I read them surreptitiously and with a good deal of speculation.

As the day moved on, the people settled into neighborhood or family groupings. Sounds blended in a resonance that hung in the warm air like a melody—voices, laughter, cries of babies, movements of people, the merry-go-round, and the sudden sharpness of a cap gun or firecracker on the outskirts. This was a splendid part of the day, a gentle drowse in the midst of so much delight.

Gossip was exchanged at the picnic and some of it originated there. If a man had taken a drink, if a couple was quarreling, if children were being abused by a stepmother or stepfather, if a girl had "got into trouble," these things had a thorough going-over. A few women, self-appointed custodians of decorum, paid particular attention to young couples, noting any prolonged absence, especially if they had been seen strolling into the woods. Girls who went to the Iconium Picnic with their beaus were solemnly warned "not to leave the crowd." A drunk or two were reported sleeping it off in the woods and now and then a fistfight would ignite, but the Iconium Picnic generally was a peaceful, well-behaved gathering.

Toward evening people would begin to talk about going home, but most of them stayed to eat what was left from dinner and call it an early supper. With supper out of the way, they said, they would not have to make a fire at home and could get right at the chores.

About that time, when the woods were cooling with lengthening shadows, a fiddler would run off a few practice notes while a rough platform was being thrown together for dancing. I had never seen anybody dance—dancing and card playing were considered sinful in our family—but I wanted to. Surely it wouldn't be sinful just to watch. Papa would mention women who danced—the Tipton girls down around Fairfield and the Suitor girls—with no derogatory word, but his voice trailing off in an unfinished sentence added to their fascination and mystery. I pictured them in white shirtwaists and long black skirts, their buttoned shoes flying over the coarse planks, their fair faces shining under the coronet of their pompadours and the soft light of coal oil lanterns. Not to stay and watch the dancing was one of the saddest disappointments of my life.

"Can't we stay just a little while, just once?" I begged.

Papa always answered, surprised that so foolish a suggestion should have been made, "We've got to get home and tend to the chores. Brindle's waiting to be milked. Besides, we're all tired out."

That didn't seem quite fair. I wasn't tired, even if I did go to sleep in the back of the wagon on the way home while my parents were reviewing the events of the day, or rather while my mother was. She said Grandma Childs was failing fast and this might be the last picnic she would ever see, that the poor Mullin girl was a pitiful sight, and that she saw three women who had on dresses of changeable taffeta which she heard cost a dollar a yard, then added, to nobody in particular, "Did you notice how fast my boiled ham went?"

Chapter 9: Waiting for the Clock to Strike

or serious illnesses Aunt Martha Bird was sent for. Present at most of the births and deaths in our community, she brought relief and comfort with her as she strode in the door. She was not the Aunt Martha who had married my Grandfather Bennington, but rather Aunt Martha Harriman, wife of my mother's Uncle George Bird. Their farm adjoined ours.

After she had reared a large family of her own, a daughter died, leaving two small girls. She took these grandchildren into her home. Thus, in the years I was growing up, although her older children were married and gone, there were still four young ladies in the house—her daughters, Artie and Laura, and her granddaughters, Della and Nell Harvey. It was a lively household. What seemed like wagonloads of dresses were draped over a cord across an upstairs room, and the girls would often let me put some of them on to play dress-up. Their house was about like ours, except it had one thing that ours lacked, a parlor, almost an essential with four girls to marry off.

It was my great regret that we had no parlor. I loved to slip into theirs and look through the plush photograph album, read the autograph book, and admire the crocheted doily fluffed around the base of the lamp. Lace curtains covered the windows, shaded with green blinds. In one corner of the room stood a walnut bed with a high headboard, a thick puffy featherbed, fringed white counterpane, and starched pillow shams. Across, in another corner, was an organ, bearing doilies, songbooks, cut glass vases, and a pink conch shell in which we were told could be heard the sound of the sea.

All week long that parlor stood with closed doors and drawn shades, but on Sunday afternoons it came to life. From behind a big syringa bush I watched young men ride up on horseback (both man and horse slicked up), tie their mounts to the fence, go to the side door, and knock. One of the essentials of a parlor was a separate entrance, possibly so the young man would not be diverted from his romantic mood by a glimpse of other members of the family not dressed in their Sunday best. In the meantime the young lady had been ready and fidgeting on the organ stool for half an hour.

My mother seldom allowed me to visit Uncle George's family on Sunday afternoons and, if she did, she told me not to enter the parlor. Young people, she said, did not like to be bothered by children; they wanted to be by themselves. It did no good to tell her that I never bothered them, but just sat in a chair thumbing through the album. I added that they didn't talk much anyway, but just sat and looked at each other.

A young man did not have many places to take the girl he was courting—church once a month, the Shiloh camp meeting in summer, the Iconium Picnic, an occasional pie supper at the schoolhouse, a spelling bee, or the Christmas tree. When he began calling on Sunday afternoons, there was little doubt of his intentions.

In a few years, I reflected, I would be old enough to sit gussied up in the parlor waiting to receive a beau at the side door. Then a heavy burden settled on me; *we had no parlor.* Would any young man come to see me and sit in the big room where all of the family sat? It did not seem likely. How, then, was I to get a husband? By that time I had sensed that getting a husband was a woman's prime enterprise in life.

I was somewhat relieved when our family made a start toward a parlor by acquiring an organ. Mamma talked of getting one each fall, thinking she might be able to spare enough turkey money after helping to pay the taxes and buying winter clothes. Whenever a Sears, Roebuck catalogue came, we turned to the organs and read every word of each description, confident that some day one of them would be ours. Then one fall it became a reality, a true beauty, the best in the catalogue. Most of the organs had five octaves. This was a six-octave Beckwith Grand, with little drawers and compartments all over, a mirror, lamp stands, and places for music. It came by freight; Papa went to Osceola and brought it home in the wagon. Neighbors came to help with the unloading. When it stood in the southeast corner beside a window, I concluded that nothing so fine had ever been in our house before.

Mamma taught me the notes: *F A C E* for the spaces on the treble clef, and *Every Good Boy Does Fine* for the lines; *All Cows Eat Grass* for the spaces on the bass clef and *Good Boys Do Fine Always* for the lines. I wonder now where my mother learned to play, but at the time I did not question it, for no knowledge or skill of hers surprised me. I learned to play with my right hand, then with my left, and soon was playing with both hands and forgot about a parlor and beau.

The last time I saw our organ, many years later, it stood in the same corner of the big room, but piled around it were bushels of wheat. The house had been abandoned; the organ, now falling apart, had been left behind.

I was not a brave child. In addition to being alternately compulsive and stubborn, bashful and brash, I was afraid that a horse would step on my bare feet if I went into his stall and afraid a strange cow would kick me if I tried to milk her. George called me—with good reason—a coward. The one event in which I behaved with some fortitude hardly balances the many times I did not, but it was at least an honest action and not a fantasy (in my dreams I always acted boldly and fearlessly). Reading the paper one evening, Papa disclosed that a child who had swallowed a prune seed had died. To this news I applied the simple logic that all children who swallowed prune seeds died.

Some weeks afterwards *I* swallowed a prune seed. I did not question that my fate was sealed and settled or expect that anything could be done to save me. I said nothing about my impending doom, but that evening I prolonged my usual rites; I combed Papa's hair long and sadly; I kissed my mother more lovingly; I was kind to Julia and George. I stood outside a bit to look at the stars and find the Big Dipper, perhaps for the last time, thought about Heaven and Hell and the Milky Way and my pink lawn dress in which I no doubt would be laid out in my coffin and wondered how it felt to be dead. But I uttered no word of farewell.

The next morning I was still alive and felt no pain. That day Uncle Willie and Aunt Etta Bernard and their children came and we ran riotously, playing hide-and-go-seek. When nothing happened in the days that followed, the dread of the prune seed faded and passed.

My concern had been replaced in part by an interest in the birds and bees. A growing child yearns for forbidden knowledge. My parents volunteered nothing and I asked no questions. Nobody had told them anything, and sex is not a subject on which parents are fluent. The Bible, which I read faithfully, yielded up some of the facts of life which I pieced together with information from the almanac with its gestation table. (This was after I looked up "gestation" in the dictionary.) The girls at school passed on bits they had overheard, and while they might not have been biologically accurate, at least they provided clues.

From these sources and observation I gradually picked up a few elementals. One day Papa came home and asked, "Guess who's got a new baby?" Without hesitation I answered, "Aunt Mabel," and felt my face flush when he laughed, "Now, how did you know that?" I had seen Aunt Mabel within the month.

And thus the year passed with its little crises and delights and mysteries and revelations. Watching the old year out was a ritual I observed alone with my lamp on the chair, the rug against the door. As midnight approached I read and copied my favorite poems as if they somehow needed to be preserved in the cornerstone of the old year. I wrote the names of our family—Jacob, Margaret, Julia, Zula, George—for what I thought was the last time in the year as I listened for the clock to strike, the exercise turning into an anticlimax as the old year hung on and refused to fade away despite my having completed my copying. I would start again, hoping to be on the dot as the last hour struck. It was like waiting for a train to leave after you have bid travelers goodbye and seen them aboard. If I moved around or dropped a book I would hear, "Is that you, Zula? Why aren't you in bed?"

"I'm just going," I would say.

When the New Year came, it came silently. No radio or television brought shouts of celebrants into our home. There was no sound but the ticking of the clock, none outside but a breath of wind. The New Year came silently, but it burst upon me like the dawn of creation. Never since has it seemed so dramatic. Shouting and crowds and horns and whistles have never been as stirring as sitting alone in my room, writing words on paper, listening, and waiting for the clock to strike.

Chapter 10: Growing

*T*he greater part of my family's effort went into the growing of food. Vegetables were raised in our garden; fruit came from orchard and woods; meat and milk, butter and eggs from animals we raised. My parents, my brother and sister, and I all shared in the work on our farm of woods and fields and pastures and running streams.

First was the plowing of the garden. Early in February my mother began preparing my father for the event. (She was not spurred by the arrival of seed catalogues, for we had saved our own seed from plants grown the summer before.) One morning at breakfast my mother would say brightly, "It'll soon be time to plant the garden." Then after more pointed remarks, which my father brushed aside as purely conversational, she would close in with, "Jake, I want the garden plowed." The finality of her statement was easily translated.

Bending to the need for garden plowing, my father hitched up Fred and Prince to the plow and pulled it into the garden, where Mother stood, a shawled Demeter, guarding the roots already slumbering in the ground.

"Don't get too near that fence. The hyacinths are all along there. . . . Watch out for that gooseberry bush." She knew where every plant was waiting in the ground and steered him clear of the pie plant (rhubarb), the winter onions, the horseradish, and the row of currants down the middle of the garden. It is easy to understand why a man does not move at the first suggestion of turning the soil in a garden. Give him a long stretch of field, alone and free, his own master, not a short cramped row in a place pregnant with hyacinths and overrun by women and children.

Potatoes were planted the day the garden was plowed. We all sat around a washtub cutting the seed we had saved, the choicest potatoes, into sections and always laughed at my mother's account of her first effort to cut potatoes, when she dug out the "eyes," the source of the new plant. Any household work my father shared took on the air of a holiday. The potatoes were dropped in the furrows and covered.

Now we had something to wait for.

I helped my mother place sets from the winter onions in a long row. Peas, radishes, and lettuce were planted and soon afterwards beets and beans. Every night we talked about what had been done. Our elation at planting a garden may seem strange at a time when vegetables can be bought fresh in the stores all year round, but we had not seen a leaf of lettuce or a radish since the year before—and would not see any until they grew in our garden.

What delight in those first pairs of radish leaves that pushed through the ground, followed by a darker, fuzzier pair, standing opposite each other like couples waiting to begin a dance. As the plants grew I pulled aside a little soil each day to see if any was big enough to eat. One day I would find one the size of a marble—it was never the one with the largest top—and after running into the house to obtain permission from my mother, I pulled it and there in the garden celebrated the spring rite of eating the first vegetable.

Our very first fresh food did not come from the garden, however. In early spring when a sharp wind and a warm sun were casting lots for the day, I went with my mother into the woods and pastures to gather wild greens. I often played there, but to be there with my mother looking for greens was better than playing. I learned to spot lamb's quarter, dandelion, sheep sorrel, and pokeweed, which my mother cut neatly at the ground. At times she would stop to listen to the song of a meadowlark, point out to me the flashing wing of a cardinal or a violet peeping through the winter's accumulation of leaves. Often she recited a few lines of poetry about a brook or flower. We would go home with the kettle heaped with greens. The outer leaves she discarded, the chosen portions dropped into a brass kettle to cook down "bad."

They boiled down into a dark, acrid mass with overtones of bitterness. Women could keep the talk going all day about which plants made the best greens. Some wouldn't touch poke; others said mustard ruined the flavor; others liked a touch of nettles or narrow dock. They were all weeds fit for nothing, I thought, but conversation.

We planted cucumbers and watermelons, made ridges for sweet potatoes, and set out cabbage plants. Sweet corn had already been planted and turnips would come later. Nearly every year my mother tried something new, sending away for the seed. One year it was carrots; in another she tried celery. We planted green beans and pole beans. Later in the summer when the field corn was grown, pole beans would be planted by stalks of corn. Speckled beans were grown every year from seed that had originally been brought from Indiana by a great-aunt.

Helping with seed gathering, I learned the extravagance of nature, or perhaps her insurance—for nature is more concerned with quantity than quality. The sycamore with its hundreds of pods filled with hundreds of seeds could populate the earth—small wonder it is called the Abraham tree. A milkweed shell, holding rapturous rows of white satin and brown velvet, bursts open and seeds fly away on wings of white floss. Some fall on stony ground. No matter. There are hundreds more.

Soon everything was growing. My mother would go to the garden to hoe in the cool of the morning, stopping first to survey her rich domain, the work of her hands. Whatever my mother did I wanted to do, but ahead of hoeing came weed pulling. I ridded the cabbage of "pursley," not a bad job, for both cabbage and purslane are strong individuals that bear no resemblance to each other. What I hated was to face a long row of beets: small timid plants overrun by a bold gang of weeds.

Beets are backwards, slow to come up, slow to grow, and so undistinguished that it takes close looking to know which is weed and which is beet. But beans—they pop right up, get going, and weeds think twice before pushing in. Weeding the beets seemed endless as I looked down the row, but as I worked, a transformation slowly took place. Instead of dwelling on how much remained to be done, I looked back at the neat row I had liberated.

My mother also worked in the garden in the cool of the evening and sometimes my father would take a hoe and help her. These were rare and momentous occasions that brought us all into the garden. Papa talked to Mamma about green tomato worms and pulling them off the vines while we children cavorted about in the pure joy of our Eden.

Summer was a vegetarian orgy, from the first lettuce to the last tomato. Wilted lettuce was our tossed salad, cut up with onions and radishes and seasoned with hot vinegar and bacon fryings. The first potatoes were "graveled" by digging gently around a vine, searching out large potatoes without disturbing the plant, and cooked with new peas. We ate a sharp, pink sauce made from rhubarb, that most delectable of spring fruits, the exactly right taste that said spring is here and summer is on the way. My mother took a pink stalk tipped with a curled chartreuse leaf and stood it in a glass of water.

"It's as pretty on the table as in a dish," she said.

I can remember my mother stopping sometimes in her work to listen, and saying with a strange, low, ecstatic tenseness, "That was a meadowlark!" I did not know then that for her its clear sweet whistle was a call of hope, a cry of faith, a promise of awakening.

We watched for the first watermelons to "set on" and

waited for them to grow. As one reached what seemed an enormous size and we begged to have it pulled, my mother would say, "Ask Papa. He knows when they are ready." Urged into the garden, he would thump the largest melons, look at the stems, and say, "Better wait a few days."

Wait a few days! We had waited all summer.

Then one morning the first melon was plucked and put in a tub of water to cool. When evening came we ate it on the porch, saving the rinds for the hogs. If it was red and ripe and delicious, my mother would save its seeds for the next year. If it was underripe we didn't mind. It was a watermelon and it was the first one of the year.

The garden was not only for summer eating; it had to provide for the winter as well. Beet pickles were sealed in glass and cucumber pickles put down in large stone jars. Cabbage was chopped for sauerkraut—I stood by to eat the stalks. Tomatoes were canned in tins and sealed with wax.

A bramble of red raspberries grew along the back of the garden and ended at an old cherry tree more noted for chewy gum and redheaded woodpeckers than for cherries. Strawberries grew on plants ordered from Kellogg's. Purple Concord grapes vined over an arbor. Peaches and apples held on in an old orchard. Fruit was canned and made into jams, jellies, and preserves.

Of all the things that grew, red raspberries were the best. I cannot trust myself to write temperately about red raspberries, eaten off the vine or with cream and sugar. Some fine adjectives enrich our tongue, but I have turned through the book and find none that begins to express the melting, ethereal delight red raspberries bring to taste, sight, smell, and touch. They satisfy every sense but hearing, but for that there was always a bird note or the far-off melancholy cawing of a crow.

The big push of the summer was wild blackberry picking. We were outfitted as carefully as for a safari. Mamma got us into shoes, stockings, and clothes with long sleeves. Over her arms she pulled a pair of heavy stockings with the feet cut out. No woman or girl wore overalls or trousers of any kind, but anything a person wore was light armor against the sharp briars of wild blackberries. Mamma said all the patch lacked of being a jungle was the tigers.

With every bucket we could carry, we walked to the blackberry patch to find heavily bending limbs. Greedily we stripped them and rushed on to more, calling to the others to come see. Although we had come to gather berries and had expected to find berries, a thick cluster induced the excitement of an old prospector striking gold. We became as insensitive to briars as the oriental fakir to the nails he lies on. With buckets filled, we went home, sighing for those we had to leave.

Things other than berries were brought from the woods. The first thing Mamma did was fill the washtub with salty water in which to give us a bath after we had been inspected for ticks, which had to be pulled off. The salt was to kill chiggers, too small to be attacked individually. As our fervor diminished we began to notice scratches that mapped red trails across our bodies and smarted in the salt water.

The great thing about blackberries was that, unlike gooseberries, they required no stemming, a dismal task more interminable than weeding beets and slower to be resolved than philosophy, but the bucketsful we gathered meant pies and cobblers all winter.

The end of summer brought the harvest in of the vegetables to be stored. Potatoes were dug; onions were braided into bunches and hung in the smokehouse; beans were hulled and stored in flour sacks; turnips were put in the cave outside the house. The garden would rally with September rains, but when the last fresh vegetable was eaten, there would be no more until another spring.

Women worked toward having frying chickens by the Fourth of July, but that required early hatching, which in turn depended on the maternal mood of the hens. Nothing could be done until the first one took a notion to set, probably a matter of body chemistry rather than whim, despite what the women implied.

"My hens just won't set this year," they complained.

When one announced her readiness by staying on the nest, fifteen of the choicest eggs were marked with charcoal and put into a nest of fresh hay into which powder had been dusted to control mites—minute, mindless creatures that make a chicken's life miserable. Too little honor has been accorded a hen for her faithfulness in staying on her eggs though tormented day after day by mites. A few hens would leave their nests, but then a few mothers occasionally desert their children, too.

Three weeks of steady setting and the eggs began to "pip." Wet and woeful chicks pushed out of the eggs, curled up from their oval world. A few hours under the warm feathers of the hen turned them into balls of fluff.

Setting a hen seemed something like giving a boost to creation. My sister and I, finding one brooding remote from the chicken yard, would gather eggs and secretly set her, hoping to surprise our mother with a fine flock of chickens. We watched over her, brought corn and bread scraps, but I seem to remember that these hens often left the nest before the eggs hatched. Perhaps their nonconformity, their isolating of themselves from the group, indicated a restless and unstable personality.

A hen is not very bright, but she is faithful according to her instincts, and women have judged her unjustly by their own standards. She faithfully hatches chickens that have scant chance of being her own flesh and blood, then rushes off the nest and begins scratching to make them a living. She is out with the dawn, dragging her chicks through dewy weeds in search of bugs and worms. If a rain comes suddenly she can be counted on to select the lowest ground on which to sit and hover over them. No matter how much water flows under and around her, there she stays. A hen understands duty but not gravity.

One warm summer day when it "looked like rain," my mother sent me to find a hen and her chicks and bring them to shelter. It not only looked like rain, it *was* rain, which came in a quick downpour, the perfect opportunity to do what I had long wanted to do—stay out in a storm. Wet to the skin, I conducted a leisurely search and found the hen hovering her brood in a watery fence corner.

I gathered the drenched chickens into my skirt and bore the hen home squawking under my arms. While her chicks, wrapped in an old shirt, were being dried in the oven of the kitchen stove, she ran about with fluffed feathers, clucking nervously. Soon the chicks were fluffed up like new and reunited with their anxious parent, who led them away proudly, but with no lesson learned. For a good many years after I lived in town I wondered, whenever it rained, what I should be bringing in.

Another day I learned about remorse when I stepped on a chick and heard it cry piteously as it died. I ran sobbing to my mother, carrying the warm, soft body, its bright eyes closed, its head—which barely peeked out from its downy body when alive—hanging limp.

Hawks and crows were the natural enemies of little chickens. One afternoon I saw a hawk swoop down, seize a chick and bear it, crying and pleading, into the sky, the mother hen trying to fly into the air after it, clucking frantically as its cries grew fainter and farther away. That day I learned of agonized helplessness.

Brindle, our Jersey cow, provided us with milk and butter for a dozen years. My mother had brought her as a heifer to her new home when she was married. A girl from any kind of a proper family was expected to bring a horse, a cow, and a featherbed as a dowry, though that word was never used. Brindle was a gentle cow who gave abundantly of her rich milk. One of my earliest memories is of standing by my mother as she milked a tin cup full for me to drink.

Brindle stood quietly as each child in turn learned to milk. My brother gave it scant attention. Milking was women's work. As the cow grew older she was called Old Jersey. Each year she produced a calf and each day came from the pasture and stood patiently to be milked, her great eyes as calm as the pond at evening. Even as she grew frail with years, her leadership was never questioned by the other cows . . . not even by an unstable red and white cow named Rose, who had one sharp and one blunt horn. Until she gave birth her life was placid, but motherhood threw her into a frenzy of apprehension. When we went to the barn lot to see a new calf of hers, my father stood by with a pitchfork.

He would come in from the barn some morning and say, "Guess what we've got? Old Jersey [or Rose or Daisy] has found a calf," and we rushed out to see the newborn. Calves were always found. One was found in a small lot where my brother and I had played that same day. Why, we asked ourselves, hadn't we found it?

Milk was strained into crocks and, in summer, carried to the cave to wait for the cream to rise and be skimmed for churning. The remaining clabber was set on the back of the stove for the whey to separate from the curd, the latter to be made into cottage cheese.

The cave, separate from the house, provided cool storage in summer and warm in winter. It also provided a nice little rounded hill for playing and was a refuge in time of storms. If a dark cloud arose bringing wind, my father was out scanning the sky, and, if the signs were ominous, he hustled us to the cave. If there was time he ran to the woodpile first to bring the axe, so that we might chop ourselves out if the wind hurled some heavy object, such as a house or barn, against the door. When it quieted we emerged from the cave and looked about, as Noah must have done when the ark landed on Mt. Ararat.

Butter was made in an earthen churn with a wooden dasher. Set at churning out under the big mulberry tree west of the house, I watched for the first flecks of yellow that promised the butter was on its way. If I churned too fast my mother would call out not to churn it all away. If I lagged she said I would never get butter that way. I closed my eyes, hoping they would open on a ring of butter.

Peaches and apples were spread on the porch roof to dry, safe from ground predators, with a thin cloth spread over them against pillaging by air. Laying the fruit and turning it was a job for children, one we liked, for it gave us a chance to climb to the porch roof, otherwise forbidden.

It also gave my father another source of worry. He would say as he left for the field, "Now, Mag, watch the children and don't let them fall off the roof." Other times he would charge my mother with keeping us from falling into the open curbed well or from standing by the stove to wash dishes and possibly catching our clothes on fire. He was not just a worrier, he was a compulsive worrier, often returning to repeat his message.

Chapter 11: Storing

$\mathcal{W}$hile the garden, chickens, and fruit formed peaks in our year, the true mountain was meat production. Our meat, outside of occasional game, came from our own chickens and hogs. Beef was not easily preserved. Pork could be cured by smoking. Shoats penned for butchering and mercifully unaware of plans being made for them must have felt fortunate at the extra feed that came their way. I stood by the pen and watched them eat. A hog can snap corn off the cob with a sharp staccato while looking at you with cold eyes in a way that makes you uneasy, particularly if you know he is nearing his last meal.

My father would confer with my mother. When they agreed it was cold enough for butchering, a day would be set and a neighbor asked to help, a labor paid for by a side of ribs. The day found me cringing in a closet at the sound of the shots of my grandfather's old muzzle-loading rifle, but my aversion did not prevent my enjoyment of the day's festivities or the ensuing product.

In a mixture of awe and curiosity I slipped down to the edge of the woods and saw the carcasses hanging, flat, white, and stark. The insides had been piled into a tub and later in the day my mother would remove the fat for rendering into lard. By evening each crock and pan bucket on the property was filled either with chunks of fat or lean pieces of pork to be ground into sausage.

These years afterwards I remember my mother in an old coat and fascinator standing in the cold, pulling off the entrails with her bare hands—my mother who lifted her face at the song of a meadowlark and made a bouquet out of a stalk of rhubarb! Hams, shoulders, and sides were salted and hung in the smokehouse to be cured with hickory smoke. Ribs, backbone, and tenderloins were for immediate eating. Liver, kidneys, and other organs thought inedible made a feast for the cats, and we always had a great many.

Supper was always late on the butchering day, but worth waiting for. I have eaten in famous restaurants, but I have found no meal so memorable as fresh tenderloins, brown gravy, and hot biscuits prepared by my mother. Talk flew back and forth about what had been done and what awaited doing, almost as comrades might eat together and talk of the day's battles and tomorrow's expectations.

Grinding sausage was a job brighter in anticipation than in performance. We couldn't wait to get to it after supper, but wished ourselves out of it long before it was finished. A stout plank to which a grinder was bolted was laid between the seats of two chairs. A child sat on one end feeding in meat; another child on the opposite end turned the grinder. My father had two worries about sausage making. "You kids be careful," he would say, "and don't get your hands in the grinder." And later, "Now watch out, Mag, and don't put in too much sage."

The sausage was stuffed into muslin bags and hung in the smokehouse with the other meats, suspended over a smoldering fire of green hickory. The smell of the smokehouse—meat and salt, old harness, braids of onions, sorghum in a wooden keg, a whiff of homemade soap, all blended together with hickory smoke—was a good enough smell all of itself.

A neighbor made sorghum from his own sugarcane, another occasion for a social gathering. While sucking the sap from a piece of cane, we watched a horse plodding in an endless circle to provide power for squeezing out pale juice which had a raw, musty smell until it was boiled down in a long shallow vat. It was stirred constantly with what looked like a wooden hoe.

We took a jugful home and later bought a kegful for winter. As for good eating, there's nothing the matter with hot biscuits and fresh molasses. When I went to the smokehouse for molasses, unplugged the corncob stopper, and rolled the keg to a level at which the contents would flow out of an improvised tin spout, I learned the truth of that old saying, "Slow as molasses in January."

Lard was rendered outdoors in a big iron kettle also used to make apple butter and soap. It passed from one family to another until its ownership was almost forgotten. Borrowing was to the neighborhood what banking is to business; it created a fluid economy. There was no disrepute in borrowing, only in not returning or repaying; women never forgot who had failed to return a cup of sugar. Families with a reputation of being constant borrowers soon sank in public esteem.

To have nice, white lard required not only select quality fat, but long, slow rendering over a low fire with constant stirring. Older children were allowed—whatever we could not do was considered a privilege—to stand and stir, and again we had to be watched to see that our clothes did not catch on fire. After the lard was strained into large stone jars, a task done by my parents, what remained was dried and crisped for seasoning. It was called *cracklings*. I did not like cracklings, any more than I liked headcheese, which my mother sometimes made from various ingredients—in my opinion better left undescribed.

One morning my brother and I were galloping about on our stick horses when we were overtaken by hunger pangs. We reined in to reconnoiter. Usually we refreshed ourselves with pieces of cornbread, which we pretended to be tobacco, offering them to each other with "Have a chaw," as we had seen men do. After a trip into the house, George said, "Guess what we're going to have for supper?" and his voice evoked visions of mysteriously good things to eat. Perhaps he should have gone on the stage.

"Cornbread," he announced. That was all to the good. I loved cornbread. Then after a pause, the exactly right timing, he added, "with cracklings."

In a corner of the kitchen stood two barrels, one for flour and one for meal ground from our wheat and corn. Sometimes I went with my father to take grain to the mill. In a calico dress and bonnet, barefooted, my hair in two braids down my back, I sat proudly by him in the spring seat.

I watched the movement of the horses' muscles under their skin and saw them stiffen in a heavy pull. I noticed the easy carriage of their heads and saw their necks bend on a hill. I tried to chart the movement of a horse's four feet, to see if the hind feet stepped exactly where the front feet had stepped. I wondered if the collars felt heavy on their necks, if the steel bits pinched their mouths, if the cruppers under their tails were comfortable.

At the mill we drove up beside a high platform. The miller, white with flour, came out, let down a wide plank hinged to the platform, and wheeled our sacks into the mill.

"Reckon it'll be upwards of an hour," he shouted above the rattle of the machinery.

That gave us time to trade. We had brought eggs and butter to exchange for groceries. (A farm wife tried to "keep the table" with the proceeds from her produce.) Our butter, impressed with an oak leaf, was dumped into a big open jar of other butters. Not much was bought at the store throughout the year—sugar, tea, and coffee beans (to be ground at home), occasionally rice and raisins or prunes, spices, soda and baking powder, lamp chimneys and wicks, coal oil for the lamps, and Star tobacco, three plugs for a quarter.

For lunch, we bought a few crackers and cheese and ate them in the wagon. They never tasted quite so good at home. Back at the mill we loaded our sacks of flour and meal—the miller kept a portion to pay for the grinding—and drove home. I clutched a striped sack of stick candy my father had bought me.

Now we had flour and meal in the house, meat in the smokehouse, cabbage and apples buried with hay under a mound in the garden, root vegetables in the cave, hulled beans and dried fruit in flour sacks, fruits and vegetables in cans and jars, a tall pile of stove wood from the woods.

Our food had been grown from seed, a summer's work that brought remembered pleasure. Now it was stored away and time could be spent knitting mittens and stockings, sewing, preparing carpet rags for weaving, and mending harness.

We were ready for winter.

Chapter 12: Grown Up and Important

*T*he great day came when I was allowed to go to Harper all by myself. Harper was our nearest town and our post office, a little place with one small store. Two or three times a week my father would ride a horse across Hogle's Creek to get the mail and buy a few groceries.

I had often gone to Harper with my father, riding behind him on the horse or in front if he took two children. But now I was going all by myself, like a real lady. My mother's side saddle was put on old Fred, the gentlest of horses; he was led up to the rail fence, and I hopped on, Papa calling out a final instruction, "Now keep his head up, Hon. Don't let him stop and nibble and don't fall off in the creek." I rode forth feeling like a young pilot taking off on her first solo flight, though in this early year of the century nobody had yet heard of pilots or solo flights. I rode past Aunt Martha's house, through the timber with its stretch of smooth road, across the creek (which wasn't very deep), arrived, dismounted, and tied Fred to the hitching post.

The store was run by Uncle Johnny and Aunt Cindy Harper, titled by courtesy. It had been run by a Harper ever since anybody could remember. The Harpers lived all about, descendants of an old pioneer family. Uncle Johnny greeted me with, "Come here all by yourself?"

Groceries were arranged along one side of the store—

sugar, coffee, beans, rice, raisins, prunes—in bulk, to be weighed and sold by the pound. On the other side were bolts of calico and "domestics," straw hats, overalls (pronounced "overhalls"), and red bandanna handkerchiefs. Domestics were muslins, particularly unbleached muslin a yard wide, to be made into sheets with a seam down the middle. Women washed the sheets and spread them on the grass for bleaching, but they never attained a genuine white.

After I had bought a quarter's worth each of sugar and coffee and a box of soda and fell into a silence, Uncle Johnny brought out three plugs of Star tobacco and said offhand, "I reckon your Poppy will want some tobaccy." His graciousness and tact were worthy of a cultivated gentleman of the world.

Aunt Cindy, plump in a calico Mother Hubbard, sat in a hickory rocking chair made by Hugh Harper in his little shop, and engaged me in a conversation that was question and answer.

"How are your Mommy's chickens doing?"

I said hawks got two and I had stepped on one.

"Do you have new potatoes yet?"

I said we graveled a few, but they were not very big yet.

"Is your Aunt Marthy well?"

I said she was out feeding the chickens when I went by.

"You've got some mail," Uncle Johnny said.

The post office was in a front corner of the store.

"Here's a letter from your Uncle Frank out in Colorado. Reckon he aims to come home. And here's one from your folks in Oklahomy."

He handed the mail through the wooden bars of the post office, along with the *Christian Herald* and *Farm and Fireside,* our two weekly papers. Before I left, Uncle Johnny handed me a striped poke of stick candy, murmuring, "Your Poppy always gets you some candy." I mounted the horse from the stile block and felt grown up and important. I had transacted business and talked woman talk.

Adding to the pleasure of my first trip to Harper was bringing home the letters. We did not get many letters, mostly letters from Uncle John and Aunt Laura and their family in Oklahoma. Uncle John's letters began, "Dear Brother and Family—I take my pen in hand to answer your most kind and welcome letter. This leaves us well and hope it finds you all the same." It continued with news of crops and prices and family and ended, "Your Affectionate Brother." The letters were in a fine Spencerian hand. Both Uncle John and my father had been school teachers. Addressing an envelope was called "backing a letter."

The *Christian Herald* and *Farm and Fireside* brought some of the outside world into our home, mostly moral and agricultural. When a rural route was started out of Quincy, we took a small daily paper. I read about the education of Helen Keller, the marriage of Alice Roosevelt to Nicholas Longworth—a full-page picture of Alice (the cover of the *Christian Herald*) was on our wall—the marriage of Princess Ena and King Alfonso of Spain, the shooting of Stanford White, the Russian-Japanese War, and the energetic regime of Theodore Roosevelt. Appeals from the *Christian Herald* to help flood and famine victims on the other side of the world moved Mamma to send dollar bills away in letters, and she contributed regularly to saving the heathen in foreign lands.

The *Christian Herald* printed sermons by Dr. Charles M. Sheldon and Dr. T. De Witt Talmage and articles by Helen Keller. Those names became as familiar to us as the names of neighbors, but at the same time they were as remote as Ruth and John the Baptist.

Years later, when I lived in Topeka, Kansas, I got to know Dr. Sheldon quite well and was a member of his Central Congregational Church, although he was no longer its active minister. I met and talked with Helen Keller when she came to lecture and met a granddaughter of Dr. Talmage. Something of the old magic came back in the presence of these people I had known in a newspaper when I was a small girl. Could it be possible that I was touching their hands and hearing their voices?

Chapter 13: The Lost Year

"This is Zula's lostyear." Mamma made it sound like one word. It was the year I was eight, the fall that Julia, George, and I all came down with whooping cough. Julia and George were soon back in school, but my cough held on. By the time I was well, our six-month school had ended. I did not agree that it was a lost year. My spirit had greened and blossomed in the loving care given me by my parents. I read it in their faces, heard it in their voices, and saw it materialize in ways that ranged from quail to quilting.

I sat enthroned in the big rocking chair spread over with an old comforter. Most days it was by the kitchen stove, near where Mamma was working, and on chilly mornings another quilt was spread over my lap and tucked in. Mamma rubbed me with turpentine, lard, and coal oil. She swathed my throat in a flannel cloth, changed regularly, changes I welcomed for the comforting rush of cool air. A sticky cough syrup was given at intervals, and Papa dosed me with quinine, removed from a blue bottle on the clock shelf with the tip of his pocketknife.

Aunt Martha Bird came and, as my cough grew worse, the doctor was sent for. He thumped and prodded, listened to my breathing, and said the whooping cough had gone into bronchitis. Neighbors came, listened to my coughing, and said to take care of that child. Plainly they doubted I would last out the winter. Brews from honey, roots, and bark were suggested, but the treatment most often recommended was rock candy soaked overnight in whiskey, then held in the mouth until it melted. Papa was opposed to whiskey. Not a drop was in our house.

News of the sickness traveled fast and, in addition to any concern that might be felt for the person who was ill, provided a touch of dramatic interest to the neighborhood. One day a man knocked at the door, stamped snow off his feet, and after exchanging some talk with my father, asked if the little one's ear ached. A sure cure, he said, was to blow smoke into the ear, adding, in explanation of the pipe he pulled from his pocket, "I knowed Jake didn't smoke." Mamma said I did not have any earache.

One morning Aunty Fanny Feaster, aunt only by neighborhood courtesy, came and, after the usual greetings, said she had "brought somethin' for the young one's cough," about which she had heard from her cousin. Modestly turning aside, she lifted her long black skirt and from a pocket in her petticoat brought out a bottle filled with liquid as dark as the inside of a blackberry. She had made it herself from herbs, some grown in her garden and some gathered in the woods and pastures.

"What that child needs," she said, "is to cut that fleem and get it out of her throat."

Hidden under shapeless underlayers of clothes, Aunt Fanny's figure had run together in the sexlessness of age. Thin gray hair was pulled back from a face carved by time, weathered by wind, and browned by the sun. Her dark eyes, the irises rimmed with narrow opalescent rings, burned with what in later years I was to know as the final truth.

She stayed for dinner and helped with the housework, talking with a quaintness I had never heard before. She wiped away her tears as she spoke of a son who had died in the summer—"He's loose from his misery and I've been caught in the weeping wheel." Heaven was mentioned with as much familiarity as though it was just across the street.

"Visitin' has perked me up," she said. "Time can be awful pokey for us old ones." She picked up the dried peaches my mother gave her and said at the door, "Now look well after the young one. They're the *enambel* of life."

Papa expressed his concern with quail. He was not a hunter. Once or twice a year he would shoot a squirrel, rabbit, or wild turkey, but when a child was sick, he thought the delicacy of quail should be provided. He brought down his father's old muzzle-loading rifle, which lay on the floor upstairs, and the powder horn and bullet pouch which hung on nails above it. He cleaned the barrel with small squares of cloth laid over the end of the ramrod, poured powder into the barrel, pushed a bullet down, and went to the meadow to look for a quail. He took powder, bullets, and ramrod with him. If a second shot was needed, the loading would have to be repeated. Toward evening he returned with two quails. Their little heads drooped down gently, their gray throats stretched out long and limp, the wing features soft and dark. Papa handed them to me, their bodies still warm. Mamma scalded them in hot water, plucked off the feathers, and cooked them in butter. We all had some for supper.

When Julia and George first went back to school I waited impatiently for them to return with news of the day—who got a headmark, who had to stand on the floor, and did anybody ask about me? I wanted to know what lessons were studied, what games played. But as time went on I began to feel a closer interest in home than in school. Allied with my parents, I regretted to hear the children returning from school to invade the closeness of our day-long world. For the first time since I had started school I was seeing and being a part of what was happening at home during the day. Mamma and I shelled garden seeds to save for next year's planting. Peas and beans were stripped from pods, radish seeds peeled from "horns," tomato, melon, and cucumber seeds rubbed loose from the papers on which they had been spread to dry. Color and odor lingered in marigold and zinnia seeds. Each kind of seed was folded in a paper and labeled.

"You'll never plant all them seeds, Mag," my father said.

"I don't reckon I will," Mamma said, "but there's always people who want seeds and sometimes we have a failure."

The kitchen was the center of activity. Mamma brought in the washtub, rubbed clothes on the washboard, boiled, rinsed, and blued them. Then she went outside and hung them on the clothesline, sometimes on days so cold they froze as they were being pinned to the wire. She came in with misery on her face. I helped with the ironing, glad to be out of the rocking chair.

Papa brought in harness to mend, splicing broken leather with copper rivets. On cold nights he warmed the bridles. Cold metal, he said, would tear a horse's mouth. He got out the last and mended shoes, cut half soles and put them on. Rips were sewn stronger than new with beeswax-reinforced twine, using two needles poked through the holes in a double stitch.

That winter Papa made an axe handle. I did not then appreciate his skill in hewing it out of a length of hickory he brought from the woods, much as a sculptor carves a figure from a block of marble. With hatchet, rasp, and knife he shaped the long graceful curve and smoothed it with pieces of broken glass, so hands would slide easily without splinters when the axe was used. The most difficult part was fitting the axe tightly into the handle, so it would not fly off in vigorous chopping. A person with a quick temper was said to "fly off the handle."

Mamma knitted woolen stockings and mittens, mended and sewed. She made me a green box-pleated skirt with black sateen suspenders that had pointed tabs over the shoulders. She went all-out for the tabs that year, put them on a brown waist for herself and on a white one for George, all neatly machine-stitched around the edges. She taught me to knit that winter.

A memory that comes back is my mother mending her coat, a brown, loose-fitting coat, the only one I remember her having in my early years. Suddenly she stopped and said to my father, "Jake, do you know how long it has been since I had a new coat?" Her voice had a tautness that indicated that more might lie beneath the surface. When she said "Jake" in that voice it meant that she was irritated, out of patience, or angry.

Best of all were winter afternoons when the rocker was moved from the kitchen to the "big room," where potato soup or ham and beans were simmering on the heating stove for supper. We sat by the fire and tacked carpet rags, Mamma and I sewing on alternate strips. She taught me, by doing, that even carpet rags must be sewn neatly and firmly.

Papa read the papers and called out bits of news, about Theodore Roosevelt and his "square deal," about the Russo-Japanese War—he was on Japan's side—and trusts, labor unions, and tariffs. "It says here, Mag," he called out, "that this woman has got the purtiest back in the world." Then, preparing to be scandalized, as he was by any unusual exposure of the flesh, he looked again and concluded, "She does have a nice plump back."

Some days instead of reading he played the French harp or gave me problems in arithmetic, which he considered the basis of all learning. I went through my reader several times and knew all the poems by heart. Mamma knew them too. She sang old ballads, "The Gypsy's Warning," "The Letter Edged in Black," "The Baggage Coach Ahead," "Annie and Willie," "Save My Mother's Picture from the Sale." Mamma had a nice singing voice. As Christmas came, her ballads changed to carols.

Christmas came quietly. Our stores had no lavish decorations. Candy canes were the first heralds. Mindful of the Bible story, I visualized the manger birth, picturing the manger in a deep narrow triangle, such as ours. The hayloft seemed a better place.

Mamma had kept a turkey from the Thanksgiving sale especially marked for Christmas. He strutted proudly about the yard and I felt a distant sorrow that he was marked for killing, but watched with interest as he was stuffed and dressed. Papa always asked Mamma to go easy on the sage. Early Christmas morning the turkey was put into the oven.

The night before Christmas after Papa had gone to the barn for his nightly rounds, he wound the clock and announced it was bedtime. We hung our wool stockings over a chair near the stove and went upstairs to bed. I lay thinking about that glorious song of old and wondered if it would come on the midnight clear tonight, but by midnight I was sleeping too soundly to have heard any song.

Morning did not bring a mass of toys. Each stocking held an orange and a sack of candy, with a striped candy cane peeping out of it. Each child had something that was bought and something that was made by our parents. It was pure rapture to find a beautiful bisque doll sitting in the chair by my stocking. Julia had a set of little dishes, no plastics, but real china. And George had a little train. It was a special Christmas. Our gifts were usually simpler, a little iron, a silk handkerchief, a locket (Julia's was heart-shaped, mine round), a small vase. One year we had little plates with the alphabet and a pictured nursery rhyme. We kept these things and cherished them for years.

Each of us had a pair of red mittens held together by that wonderfully ingenious idea of a cord that could go through the sleeves of a coat. One year Mamma knit me a pair of gloves with fingers and colored stripes across the hand. She made a ball for George, tightly wound twine sewed through firmly and covered with leather. She cut two figure-eight pieces from old gloves and sewed them around the ball. Papa and Mamma never gave each other anything for Christmas. Christmas was for children.

Uncle Willie and Aunt Etta Bernard and their children, Fratie, Fresca, and Lowell, came for dinner. We had fun playing with the new toys while the women, aprons over their long dresses, worked in the kitchen and the men sat by the fire and talked. Then came the dinner. People who have dining rooms do not know the sensuous pleasure of eating in the room where the food is cooked. Adding to the taste was the smell of turkey and gravy, of spice and seasoning, of fresh-baked bread and perking coffee. Food was passed around; more was brought from the stove; and the meal ended with the pumpkin pie, not served in a separate plate, but passed around in its tin for each to take a piece.

After dinner we played again while the women washed the dishes and the men dozed by the fire. When the company left we played with our new toys until Papa wound the clock and said it had been a long day and it was time for bed. We went reluctantly. I wanted to take my doll to bed—I named her Rosy Cosette—but Mamma said I might roll over and break her, an unthinkable calamity.

I lay in bed peaceful and happy. I had not heard the angels sing, but I had been touched by love, which is the magic of Christmas, and as I fell into a dreamless sleep the silent stars went by.

Chapter 14: Needed Things

*W*arm days came, bringing plans for plowing and planting. They also brought the seasonal visits of peddlers. The advent of a peddler was something to think about for days. Peddlers traveled in a buggy, always men, whom we remembered as short and stout and—despite the loneliness of back-country roads— jolly and jovial. They brought gaiety and excitement into weathered farmhouses and were never denied admission.

Out of their big, battered telescopes, held together by two leather straps, poured a stream of laces, ribbons, embroidery, hairpins, buttons, scissors, fringed shawls, little vases, mugs, children's plates, kitchen knives and small tools, needles and pins, even lengths of dress material, bright things to entice women who had so little brightness in their lives. We gathered around as the peddler spread his wares, hoping Mamma would buy something. A Magical Top that spun on a string came from the peddler's pack and lasted a long time. We remembered the way he wound it, pulled the cord away suddenly, set it spinning, then stood back and said admiringly, "I'm here to tell you that thing warbles."

If it was dinnertime, a peddler was asked to stay and eat. In return he reduced the price of an article that Mamma had lingered over or gave some trinket to a child. Peddlers slept at the farmhouses, too, for no hotels were available short of the county seat.

Mamma bought some ribbon and lace, a package of bone hairpins, a paring knife, a comb, and several packages of shoelaces. We were delighted at the purchase of any bright frippery from a peddler, but nothing brought as much solid satisfaction as shoelaces. Much of my childhood seems to have been entangled with getting my shoes laced. The first time a string broke it was nothing at all. It could be tied and made as good as new. Even the second break was not a calamity. But when it was worn to the breaking point and the tips began to come off, a frail shoestring could cloud a child's life.

A farmer was not going to hitch up the horses and go to town for a shoestring, but he could provide a substitute, a length of twine, twisted, doubled, twisted again, then rubbed with beeswax. The child who needed the shoestring took one end of the twine and helped twist. The knot tied in the ends was hard to get through the holes, particularly if the metal eyelets had come off. At such a time a nice new pair of shoestrings with tips that went right through the flabby holes—well, no bright frippery could compete with ease and comfort.

Peddlers had little trouble selling. They supplied needed things like hooks and eyes, needles and pins—"I'm all out and haven't been able to get to town"—or bright novelties that gave pleasure, all affordable. But the real hotshot salesmen were the picture enlargers. They knew the vulnerable spots and never missed one. The standard pitch was for enlarging pictures of parents and an even more surefire was the picture of a child who had recently died. The enlarger talked sentimentally of the dear old father who had worn himself out with the hard work he did for his children and of the sainted mother who went down into the valley of death for them. Then he paused to allow the message to take hold. After exactly the right length of silence, he asked gently, "Are your dear parents living?" If they were, he said how proud they would be to see their pictures hanging in their dear daughter's home. If they were not living, it was all the more reason why they should be looking down from the walls, big as life and twice as solemn. Pictures were hung, not at eye level, but considerably above. Then, of course, the husband's parents must not be neglected. They too had worked hard and gone down into the valley. The amount of the down payment was skillfully negotiated—high enough to close the deal, but low enough to be acceptable. Then frames were needed and the sharpest peddlers sold enlargements in odd shapes that would not fit any ordinary frame that might happen to be around the house.

A final event of my lost year was a quilting party on my birthday, the second of March. Mamma had set me to piecing a quilt, my first and my last, a simple quilt with blocks of nine squares. A lining made of two lengths of white muslin was sewn into the quilting frames, then covered with cotton batting, and the pieced top sewn to the lining. Neighbors and relatives were invited to come by and spend the day. They brought needles and thimbles and sat along the sides, quilting a comfortable "reach," then rolling the frames for another. The usual jokes were made, including the one that my future husband would get his toenails tangled up in my big stitches. Mamma cooked a good dinner of chicken and dumplings and, when the last narrow panel was almost finished, the women began to talk about going home. A few said they would stay until it was finished. The pleasure of the day spilled over into the next, when Mamma and I bound the edges of the quilt. We pointed out squares of all our dresses, bright as the day the materials came out of the store, pieces even of the very ones we were wearing, faded from sun and suds. As a museum of family clothing, the quilt took on new importance.

With the coming of spring my cough had gone and I took my usual place in the family again. One thing was certain. It was not a lost year. How could it be when I had been so loved and nurtured, had a beautiful doll and a special quilt of my own making?

Chapter 15: School

*T*he first thing I remember about school is sitting under the mulberry at the front gate waiting for Julia to come home and tell me what happened during the day. Julia was small and quick and bright. When she talked, words tumbled over each other, sounding like water running over the rocks in the branch in our pasture. She was quick to make up her mind, quick to act. In later years I thought of her as beautiful. Her hair was dark blond and her eyes blue, but it was her golden skin that gave her a special glow, skin that was pale gold, transparent, and very much alive. I think of her now as goodness. We all loved her.

Also, I wanted to see if anything was left in her dinner bucket. A biscuit that had been to school was much more desirable than one fresh from the kitchen. When the lid was pried off, a strange smell leaped out—of biscuits and fried meat, cookies and apples that had been shut up together all day in a half-gallon syrup pail.

Union School was half a mile from our house. The road skirted the woods, curved around the hogpen, crossed the little branch between our house and Uncle George Bird's, eased up a sloping hill, turned sharply north—and there was the schoolhouse, a weather-worn, one-room, wooden building. The weedy playground was unfenced (there was nothing that needed to be kept out) and the only accoutrements were the two little houses out back, a curbed well with a tin bucket, and a neatly stacked rick of wood.

The door was on the east side, and just inside was a shelf for dinner buckets and nails for coats. Behind the teacher's desk at the west end was the blackboard. Each side of the room had three windows. Pupils sat at double seats graduated in size from front to back and well marked with contemporary carving. Girls sat on the north, boys on the south, and either sat in the middle row, which was broken by the stove in the center of the room, its long pipe making a right-angled turn before it entered the flue.

The school term, six months long, began the first Monday in August, by which time farm work had slacked and there were a few months before the older boys would be needed to help with corn cutting. By the end of January school had closed, in time for spring work. Young men and women, up to and around age twenty, often attended school for a part of the term when there wasn't much else they could do.

Each district ran its own school with little help or hindrance from outside. As opening day approached, mothers went to the schoolhouse to wash windows and clean up the accumulated dust of six months. Then the teacher took over. She was in charge and, if she couldn't run the school, she did as an unsuccessful prime minister does—she resigned.

On the first day she announced the rules: no whispering, only one person was to be out of the room at a time, and no one was to leave the playground without permission. An experienced teacher knew she would be tested on two counts, and how she passed them was more important than the kind of certificate she held. The tests were in discipline and knowledge.

The big boys began provoking her with small, then larger, misbehavings to see how much she would put up with and whether she had the nerve to whip them. Kids would go home and tell their parents that a certain boy got a whipping and that he just stood there and laughed at the teacher.

One year the boys in another district had run two teachers

out of school before Christmas. Then a third came: a spunky little woman—everybody said they ought to have hired a man—who oozed authority. Without laying on a hand, any of the rowdies could have tossed her over the schoolhouse, but she brought order to the school. It was the news of the year. Men in wagons met in the road, stopped to talk, offered each other a chew of tobacco, and shook their heads in admiration. "Don't know how she done it, little bitty thing like her."

The other test was trying to stall a new teacher in arithmetic. A favorite was the last of 180 problems in Milne's *Arithmetic*, about A, B, and C buying a grindstone together. How much, it was asked, would each (given the dimensions of the stone) need to grind off to use up his third? This made no sense in a place where every farmer had his own grindstone which lasted a lifetime or longer. (My father's grindstone is now a rock in our patio.) By the time A had ground off his share, B and C would be in more need of a tombstone than a grindstone.

Teachers had standing in the community. There was little wealth or class. About everybody felt equal to everybody else, with the teacher and preacher at the top of the social ladder and a few slothful families down below. We grew up thinking school was the most important thing in a child's life, and we tried never to miss a word in spelling or fail to have our lessons. Papa helped us at night, encouraged us to excel, and we were never kept at home to help with work. He had been a teacher himself.

My first teacher was Miss Minty, Minty Crump, and when I cried on the first day she gave me a tiny *Piso* almanac. Miss Minty had a smooth, dark pompadour and a long, black skirt that swung out at the bottom like a bell. She wore white waists with high collars and long sleeves and wore a watch on a gold chain around her neck. I sat and watched the chain make describable loops and parabolas from its diamond-shaped clasp as she bent to help a child with a problem or stooped to put a stick of wood in the stove. I observed every motion of her skirt, every tuck and fold of her blouse, the way she sat with both feet at the side of her chair, like riding sidesaddle, her hand touching the bell on her desk. She was beauty and grace, goodness and wisdom, and I would have loved her even without the *Piso* almanac.

Teachers boarded in the district and during the term were invited to spend a night in the homes of pupils, often to sleep with one of the children, for houses were small. These visits were important occasions. It made you feel good to sit and listen to your parents talking to your teacher with none of them mentioning any of your faults or failures. If popcorn balls and molasses candy were made during the visit, the peak was crowned. Dark molasses was pulled until it turned pale amber. Although usually it wasn't cooked long enough and was sticky, nothing could mar the glory.

It carried over into the next day when the teacher's dinner was packed in your bucket and you sat beside her at her desk to eat lunch. My mother always fried ham and made a pie. I wondered if I ought to take something and hand it to her or ask her to help herself, the polite thing to do when there was company at home. She took hold of the situation and a sandwich at the same time, broke the latter, and handed half to me. If I had been struck dead at that moment my life would have been full to bursting.

When I went to school George was left at home to play by himself. The next year, when he was five, he went for a day to visit, as young children often did. He decided that school was for him—he was not one to cry on the first day—and made such a fuss to be allowed to go again that he was sent regularly. We were very proud of him at school, a handsome, lively child with curly blonde hair, natural and free with everybody. I can see just how he looked, in knee pants and "swag waist." (The latter was a shirt that bloused at the waist, with a drawstring, and buttoned down the front. At each side of the front closing and around the collar was ruffled embroidery. The drawstrings were always coming out of George's waists and having to be run in again with a darning needle worked backwards.) When he came home the first day he said, "They laughed at me and Miss Grace told them to hush." The teacher that year was Grace Fester. George was never timid or embarrassed, a delightful child.

By contrast, I was both bashful and stubborn and still cannot understand an incident in which the two added up to an unbelievable defiance of authority. Being stood on the floor near the teacher's desk was a punishment for small offenses. One day I was shocked to hear Miss Grace say, "Zula, you may bring your book and come to the floor." I might have been whispering. I do not remember my misdeed.

Miss Grace's "may" was too polite a word. I had never been stood on the floor or been punished in any way. The thought of exhibiting myself like a witch in a pillory, publicly disgraced, was unbearable. This feeling was stronger than my training in obedience. I sat in my seat sullen and silent. Miss Grace advanced toward me to enforce her order. I slid to the other side of the double seat and held on tight, determined not to be taken. She walked sedately around the row of seats to the other side and I slid back again, making far more spectacle of myself then if I had gone quietly to the floor instead of being dragged there. Miss Grace gave up our little game of dodge, reached across the seat, pulled me up and marched me to the pillory, where I faced the wall and felt my shame visible to the tittering children.

An even more painful incident came a few years later. Herbert Keller had been telling around that I was his girl, and I declared I was no such thing. My best friend and seatmate, Jessie Harper, and I, in what might be called privy council, composed this verse:

> The apple is yeller
> I throwed it in the cellar
> To get it good and meller
> For Herbert Keller.

After school took up we read it to ourselves, giggled and whispered, so pleased with our composition that we did not see the teacher as she bore down on us and took the piece of paper. She read it aloud to all the school. Our humiliation was so great that we were not heartened by the shrieks of laughter that greeted the verse. Herbert seemed pleased to have a poem written about him, and we were stood on the floor, a sad reward for our creative effort.

A child who wasted time drawing pictures or writing poems was liable to be punished. No foolishness could be tolerated; school was for book learning. But it was also for playing. We loved recess, and noon was even better. Dinner was eaten quickly and we ran out to play with the last bites in our mouths. We played Work-Up, Dare Base, Shinny, Andy-Over, and, when it snowed, Fox and Geese. There were other games, Drop the Handkerchief, Crack the Whip, London Bridge—how could a person choose between peach and apple, silk or satin, or gold and silver?—and the singing and partner games, such as Miller Boy and Skip to My Lou.

We played with a concentrated passion that engaged mind and muscle, heart and nerve. Every thought and feeling, wish and hope was focused with burning intensity on getting to the base safely, on having the handkerchief dropped behind us, or on catching the ball. We played with that powerful flowing energy which fuses into a singleness of purpose in instances of great pleasure or great danger. The sound of the bell went through us like a physical pain.

Almost as much fun as playing were spelling and ciphering, which we did Friday afternoons after the last recess. Two pupils named to "choose up sides" guessed at the page of a book the teacher held open and the one nearest right had the first choice. The two sides faced each other and spelled words alternately. Anyone who missed a word sat down—until only one was left standing.

When we ciphered, a child from each side, beginning with the smallest, went to the blackboard and the teacher gave a problem. Each pupil coming to the board could choose the kind of problem he wanted, provided the other had covered that portion of the arithmetic in class. The one who first got the correct answer took on the next person of the opposing team. Chalk dots were made fast and furiously as columns were added.

The last Friday of the month was a day when one or more directors came to school with the teacher's warrant. When my father, a member of the board, came, the children looked at me and grinned. I grinned back, pleased at the distinction. He had taught Union School before he was married, when as many as sixty pupils jammed into the room, and he added algebra classes for the older ones. Teachers always asked the directors if they had anything to say. They seldom did, but one Friday when we were ciphering Papa responded to the invitation by going to the blackboard and showed the pupils how to add without making dots.

A child likes to have his parents around, but he wants them to blend into the scenery, to act like everybody else's parents, and here was my father standing at the blackboard acting like a teacher. Yet even in my embarrassment I felt proud of him. The children went on making dots when they added. Putting numbers together in their heads was too much work.

Spelling was as much a community entertainment as athletic contests are now. Crowds gathered when two schools had a spelling bee. The pupil who could spell everybody down (and it was usually a girl) was the equivalent of the homecoming queen. I was proud to bursting when Julia, not nearly as big nor as old as most of the others, stood up and spelled the house down.

School was the scene of many pleasures, but none was greater than wearing new shoes—new shoes that squeaked. Children came to school barefooted until the weather turned nippy; then they were taken to town and fitted with shoes. A child with squeaky new shoes made many trips to the teacher's desk and to the water bucket and to sit in front of the fire. And, of course, it was expected that every child would try to spit on them, for not to have your new shoes spit on was as humiliating as for a newly married couple not to be given a charivari.

One thing a girl yearned toward as she grew up was a corset. Mamma made my first corset. She cut shaped sections from unbleached muslin called "domestic," using stays, hooks, and eyes from an old corset of hers. I had about as much figure as a fence post and an equal amount of feminine allure, but, encased in my corset, I felt as curvaceous as Lillian Russell. I minced up to the teacher's desk, certain that everybody in the room must know I was laced and stayed. Because I was practically straight up and down and because it was not anchored to my stocking with supporters, the corset gradually worked up till it poked me under the arms. But for them, it would undoubtedly have come off over my head. Women's corsets at that time did not have supporters. Stockings were held up with elastic garters or, in an emergency, with string.

Children learned things at school not mentioned in books. Mothers, having been told nothing themselves, told their daughters nothing. I learned about the "monthlies" from older girls at school and the knowledge was a secret burden for many weeks. One of them said, and it seemed slight compensation for what must surely be an intolerable cross, that it "made a girl lots prettier."

Ellen was about thirteen, a few years older than I. She had big dark eyes, a clear white skin, and black braids crossed over her head. She was large for her age with round breasts and a figure. When the boys caught her in Blackman they held her a little longer than was necessary and she had to wiggle loose. She lived with her mother, stepfather, and several younger brothers and sisters. She was like any of the other girls at school, running and playing, when she suddenly became the center of a mystery.

She stopped coming to school. For some reason, the usual inquiries were not made of whether she was sick or her mother was ailing. I sensed something different about her absence. One day two women came to our house and talked with my mother in lowered tones that gave off sparks of anger. One of them, a cousin of Ellen's mother, mentioned the stepfather's name and said bitterly, "He ought to be run out of the country."

That was a clue. Had Ellen's stepfather given her a hard whipping? If he had, it would have been talked about. If a child was whipped severely there was angry talk about the neighborhood about "welts on that boy as big as a buggy whip." Although whipping was an acceptable form of punishment, parents would threaten a child, "I'll whip you till the blood runs down to your feet," not meaning a word of it. Papa seldom punished us and, when he did, he spanked. Mamma's frail peach switch left little impression, physically or psychically. All my life the sight of physical violence, whipping more than any other, has been disturbing.

I was sure Ellen's stepfather had not whipped her, however. I thought about it, puzzled over it within the furthest range of my knowledge, and could find no answer. But I did not dare ask. I sensed it was something children were not supposed to know.

School lasted through the hottest and coldest days of the year. Two or three times in the drowsiness of a hot day a boy would hold up his hand and ask if he could "pass the water around." He brought a bucketful from the well and carried it from seat to seat, each child drinking from the dipper. Among the many things we had never heard of were germs.

We walked to school in cold that penetrated several layers of underwear, home-knitted wool stockings, fascinators, caps, and coats. There was a morning when I became so cold on the sloping hill that I sat down and cried. Julia made me get up and go on again.

When a heavy rain sent the little branch swirling across the road, walking to school was an adventure. If it was really high, Papa took us to school on old Fred, one child sitting in front of him and one or two behind. If a heavy rain fell during the day he came to school after us.

It was expected that every year a teacher would have a pie supper or box supper to get money for maps, a dictionary, or new library books. (I cannot remember when I learned to read—it was before I went to school. Julia may have taught me.) Our school's library consisted of twenty to thirty books piled on a triangular shelf in a corner (the same corner where children were stood for misbehaving). I read them all and repeated most of them. It was there that I first learned of Shakespeare through a man named Lamb. There was a translation of Vergil's *Aeneid*, poems of Matthew Arnold, Longfellow, and Tennyson, and a story about Koonah, an Eskimo boy. I wept over the fate of Evangeline and Gabriel and the tragedy of Sohrab and Rustum and was charmed by the fantasy of a strange girl who walked on the bottom of the ocean. I read the old fairy tales and learned that everything always comes out right in the end, the good rewarded, and evil punished.

A program of recitations, songs, and "dialogues" was given before the pies or boxes were sold. Pupils learned pieces, then learned to say them "with gestures." A child would report to the teacher, "I know my piece and I'm ready for gestures now." In one dialogue, Julia was supposed to faint and be carried to a coach. Embarrassed at the idea of being carried, she arose, walked to the coach, then lay down, and permitted herself to be revived. Julia was quite good one year in "Annie and Willie's Prayer," and I was proud of George when he recited four lines, rapidly with spirit, and brought the house down. He was an adorable little boy, though I never heard anybody use that word to describe him. I loved to speak pieces and always chose a tale of heroic tragedy. In the years since I was in Union School, I have seen some of the world's most renowned actors on stage, but I cannot bring myself to be critical of those pie supper entertainments, bound round as they are with the tender grace of nostalgic memory.

Sheets brought from home and strung on a wire across the end of the room curtained a stage. Parents carried coal oil lamps to the schoolhouse for the evening and it was strange to see the familiar room by lamplight, shadows held back by soft yellow ovals of light. No actress on opening night could have been more fidgety and feverish than those pupils were as they darted back and forth under the ends of the curtains while waiting for the program to begin.

Then came the main event of selling the boxes. Girls sewed them in fancy shapes of hearts, diamonds, and circles and flossied them up with crepe paper ruffles. A girl always let her "regular feller" know which box she had brought and it was good sport to "run the box up" to make him pay a higher price. A young man considered it a compliment to have his girls' box bid up, but at one box supper a young man with a practical turn of mind dropped out of the bidding and let the runner-up eat with his girl. The buyer was not prepared for such a turn and had to borrow money to pay for the box.

Bidders generally bought a box and took their chances. Sometimes it turned out to be a married woman's. Sometimes a man, if the bidding was slow, bought two boxes and ate with two girls, neither of whom considered it an altogether cozy arrangement. One young man was a little less than gracious when he discovered that the box he bought belonged to a little girl so bashful she had to eat sitting on her mother's lap.

I was not that girl. I was too bashful to take a box until I was much too old to sit on my mother's lap. The one I took to the last box supper I attended at Union School was bought by Frank Tuck, who had asked Julia to signal him when it was up for sale. Frank and I stood behind the middle row of desks at the front of the room and ate, consuming fried chicken as daintily as possible and biting from the pointed tips of the pieces of apple pie. Amid the hum of voices, we ate in self-conscious silence, the warmth of Frank close beside me. After we had finished he said, low and hurried, "May I see you home tonight?"

Frank was the nicest boy in school, tall and good-looking, and I liked him better than any other, but it was the first time a boy had asked to see me home. In a panic of shyness, I mumbled, "Not tonight," gathered up my box, and moved away. (Frank never asked me again, but neither did he allow the incident to blight his life. He married and became the father of six children.)

I walked home with my family, thinking new thoughts.

A boy had asked to see me home and had given me a glimpse into another world, which I knew with a certainty would have a shine more glowing than that of playhouses and doll dresses, Blackman or Shinny. My father carried a lantern and I watched the long shadow cast by his legs as the light swung with his steps, a metronome keyed to the sound made by the stiff legs of his trousers as they brushed against each other at every step. This was my own safe world, but as I walked home along the old familiar road I was thinking of a new one.

The school term closed in a burst of good will. The Last Day of School was a holiday that rated capitals and ranked close to Christmas. Parents came bringing food for a basket dinner which was spread on planks on the middle-row desks between the stove and the door. I begged Mamma to let me wear my hair hanging down on the last day of school, unbraided and falling from a ribbon tied around my head, wavy from being done up on rags the night before.

Children crowded into the front seats to make room for parents, who sat and listened to classes. Pupils read with self-conscious pride and tried not to stumble over any word. It is to the credit of the teachers that they did not ask only the better readers, but gave all a chance to be heard by their parents.

At noon the room was bustling with women setting out food, murmuring apologies for a fallen cake, with children running in and out, excited and laughing, with men around the perimeter talking as they rested one foot on the seats, and with the teacher mingling as a kind of high priestess of the occasion. Neither she nor the children had brought dinner baskets that day.

In the afternoon the teacher gave a little talk saying how much she had enjoyed the term and that she would miss the children. A director usually responded with an appreciation of her work. The day came to an end with a mingling of joy and sadness. A few children always cried to be parted from a teacher they loved. She cheered them with, "You'll have a good time this summer and we shall see each other again in the fall," or, if she was not coming back, "You'll like your new teacher."

The only male teacher at Union while we attended it was Jack Boring, who held a kind of awe for us. His family was involved in a feud with another branch of the Boring family. (A man on each side of the family had been shot and killed.) Julia had somewhat of a crush on Mr. Boring, as girls often do for men teachers. I ought to know. I married one of my teachers, but that was some years in the future.

Mr. Boring gave his pupils a little book at the end of the school year with his picture and all of our names in it, along with a poem that began (I still have my book, but I remember the poem by heart from years ago):

The Close of School

The time has come to say farewell!
    For now our term is through;
To sound our present school days' knell
    And bid you all adieu.
Farewell—a word that stings our hearts,
    That moves our feelings strong,
That sadness frequently imparts,
    And makes us linger long.
For months together we have met
    And conned our lessons o'er,
And done our best to know and get
    A part of learning's store.
Thro' all the days I've labored hard,
    And often during night;
Your progress was my sole regard,
    Your well-fare my delight.

We lingered long that day, saying goodbye to each other and gathering up our books, slates, and tablets. (Special papers were kept between double slates. Children loved to use double slates, but thrifty parents cut them apart for the use of two children. If any paper was left over it was saved for another year—a five-cent tablet was something to take care of. A pad of blank paper still gives me pleasure.) Mothers were given these things to look after while children played a last game of tag.

My last game of tag. My last Last Day of School was a sadness near unbearable, for I could not look ahead to seeing my friends the next year. Perhaps I would never see them again. That was the year I was fifteen. That was the year we moved to Colorado.

Chapter 16: The Decision

*U*ncle Frank and the Bird boys, John and Ed, had "gone out West" where the country was growing up. Uncle Frank wrote back that he was making sixty dollars a month "riding ditch," an amount that seemed riches to hill farmers of Missouri, who saw little cash during a year. The Bird boys worked on ranches in Montana, Uncle Frank in Colorado.

When anyone returned for a visit, the news spread rapidly. Neighbors gathered in the evening, sat on straight chairs or leaned against the wall to hear talk of a far country, of open ranges, cowboys, bunk wagons, and water brought down from the mountains to water crops. To men who seldom traveled beyond their own county, Colorado and Montana seemed as remote as Tibet and Siam.

Papa often talked of going to Colorado and taking us all to live there. Uncle Frank urged that the country was new, land was cheap, and jobs were plentiful. But it was neither adventure nor wealth that lured Papa. It was the belief that the high altitude was good for "lung trouble." Understood but rarely spoken was his fear of becoming a victim of the consumption that had killed his mother.

Even an ordinary decision upset my father and required encouragement and assurance from my mother. So when it came to the big one of leaving a place where he had lived more than half his life, a place where his wife and children

(Top) Seated, from left: Jacob Bennington with daughters Julia and Zula (baby); George Holley holding Sam; Christina Holley; and Willie Bernard. Standing, middle row: Margaret Bennington, Seldon Holley, Nora Holley, and Etta Bernard. Standing, back row: Will Holley and John Holley.

(Left) Zula Bennington.

Edward and Margaret Greene, photographed in 1922 or '23.

Zula with sons Edward (top) and Willard, Jr., 1928.

Written on the back of this 1936 photograph, in Zula's hand: "This is the old house in Missouri where Zula Greene was born. Standing in the yard is her daughter Dorothy. Houses at that time were never painted, just left to weather into a gray. The shadow on the house is from one of the 4 large mulberry trees in the yard."

Zula and Willard Greene, 1936.

Jacob and Margaret Bennington outside the Greenes' second
Topeka home, 1601 Mulvane.

An undated
portrait,
probably from
the early '40s.

In her home office at
1205 Mulvane.

With her cat Goodie, April 14, 1969.

With playwright William Gibson, left, and Dr. Karl Menninger.

In the early '80s.

had been born, and where he owned a farm, it threw him into an anxiety in which he popped his knuckles and walked the fields.

A wet, cold winter tipped the balance.

Rain came, slowly, steadily, and daily. It seeped into the earth and turned the barn lot into a primordial mire. Horses and cows slogged wearily through it and, when they lay down, arose caked with mud. Corn ears fed to the hogs sank into the mush. Papa struggled through it and wished aloud that he had a pair of gum boots.

"Why don't you go to Quincy and buy a pair?" Mamma asked.

"Surely the rain must be about over," he said hopefully.

"But you'll need them for the next rain," Mamma persisted.

On a morning when the rain was a cold drizzle he came in, soaked, water running off the bill of his cap and dripping down his face. He sat down beside the kitchen stove where Mamma was cooking breakfast.

"I've got the weak trembles, Mag," he said. "Fix me some quinine."

"Get those wet clothes off," she ordered. "You'll be down sick."

She brought the quinine and I ran for dry clothes, red flannel drawers and undershirt, top shirt, and pants. Papa sat in the house all day, dozing in a rocking chair, but at evening was out again in the fine mist, slogging in mud that sucked at his shoes. In the morning Papa's eyes burned with fever. Mamma put cold wet cloths on his head and sent for Aunt Martha Bird. She said he ought to see a doctor. By now we had a telephone, a party line on which our ring was three shorts and a long. People listened in and if an excuse was needed it was somebody might be sick and need help. If a thunderstorm threatened, people ran outside and unhooked the lead-in wire, so lightning would not enter the house.

A doctor was called only when a person was "real bad

sick," otherwise patience and home remedies were relied on. Mamma decided this was an emergency. The doctor came, riding horseback, sat down by the stove, and talked of things in general.

"You've got a bad case of grippe, Jake," he finally said. "That fever's up there pretty high and if you don't watch it, it could go into pneumonia."

Papa asked the question always in his mind: "Has it got into the lungs?"

"Don't seem to be. Now you take this medicine and stay in out of the weather. And, Mag, keep his chest greased with flannel rags."

The visit of a doctor was comforting. He resolved fear, real or imaginary, into a concreteness for which he prescribed a remedy. Papa and Mamma were more cheerful. A neighbor boy came to help with the chores and Papa stayed in the house, sitting in the rocking chair with his feet on another chair. He was not one to lie in bed, even when sick.

There was talk between our parents which tapered off when a child came into the room, and several things began to happen. One was plans for having a family group picture taken. Photographs were not made often or lightly. The stern or solemn faces in old pictures reflect the gravity of facing a photographer.

The day was set and we were washed, combed, and dressed in our best. Julia and I wore our white lawn dresses with the flower stripes, and big lace-edged berthas. Mamma wore her brown tab blouse, George his ruffled swag waist and knickers, Papa his Sunday suit and white shirt. And that is how the photographer caught us, one family in a moment of time and space.

At night, I combed Papa's hair, as he liked me to do. Instead of reading he would sit and look at the fire. He was feeling much better, but Mamma still put hot cloths on his chest at night. Uncle Frank, learning of Papa's illness, renewed his urging to come to Colorado. Papa decided that in the spring he would go by himself, get a job, and work through the summer to see how he liked the country and determine what his prospects might be.

The decision made, he was in better spirits and we were all excited at the approaching adventure. Albert Dietz, a young neighbor, was hired to stay with us and do the farming. Papa's clothes were packed in the telescope suitcase and we all went to take him to board the train at Osceola.

Of that summer during Papa's absence, I remember that lightning struck the barn and killed a horse and that Mamma asked all the neighbors to bring our mail when they went to Harper. Plowing, planting, and harvesting went on, but we seemed to be suspended in a glassed-in world, waiting for Papa to come home.

He brought back rings of Colorado gold for Mamma, Julia, and me. (He had not given Mamma a ring when they were married. At that time and in that place a ring was not necessarily a part of getting married.) Papa brought George a four-bladed, pearl-handled knife from which he had already ground off the sharp points of the blades. He always visualized the worst, and it came near happening one day. George fell down the stairs with the knife open. Its dull blade stabbed him just above the eye.

The decision was made that we would move to Colorado, but not as quickly as it takes to say it.

Over and over Papa would ask, "Do you think we're doing the right thing, Mag? If you don't want to go. . . "

And Mamma would interrupt with assurances that she thought it was what they ought to do.

Julia taught school that year and toward the end of the term announced that she and Albert planned to be married. It was a new anguish for Papa. He did not want her married; he had expected her to go to Colorado. She was eighteen, small, quiet, and gentle. She did not talk as much as she used to and seemed younger than she was, a child with no preparation for marriage. It was a painful time for Papa and

Mamma, breaking up our family and moving away.

Mamma made Julia a pretty wedding dress of white China silk and she was married in the Methodist church, coming forward at the end of the regular Sunday service with her attendants. That was the church wedding of the times. Most weddings were performed in the home of the bride. Relatives and friends went to the church for the wedding and came to our house afterwards for dinner, bringing presents, mostly dishes, not necessarily matched. I made a list of gifts and donors.

Julia and Albert were going to live in our house and farm the land. We left the farm animals, machinery, and furniture. Fred, Prince, and Brindle were getting old, twenty years or more, and had come to seem like members of the family. My mother packed dishes and bedding and small things. We were going to live in a house on one of Uncle Frank's farms.

It was a memorable time. We visited relatives and solemnly shook hands all around. Parting from my dear friend Jessie Harper was not a sweet sorrow; it was painful. I would go to her house, she would walk home with me, and I would walk back home with her until finally we parted halfway between.

Sniffling and red-eyed when we boarded the train at Osceola, I dried my tears in embarrassment when a young man I knew, Roland Roy Harvey, came and sat beside me. He wrote letters to me in Colorado and sent a photograph album.

The novelty of riding on a train diminished my grief. The only other time I had been on a train was when our family went to Oklahoma to visit Uncle John, Aunt Laura, and our cousins. I was four or five at the time, and my memories of that trip are of Uncle John's big windmill and of having an accident in the night and feeling shame as my mother washed me while Aunt Laura held a coal oil lamp and said, "She just ate too much watermelon."

On the train George and I passed the time eating from the big basket of food my mother had packed, going to the water cooler for a drink, and looking out the windows. Cinders drifted back from the engine and got in our eyes. Romances of the times often started with a young man whipping out a clean handkerchief, folding it into a point, and removing a cinder from the eye of a young lady who sat near him. At Kansas City we changed to the Burlington, which cut across the corner of Kansas into Nebraska and on to Denver, where we caught the Rio Grande.

We listened to the clack of the wheels and made up words to fit the rhythm.

George said it sounded like "Where the bloom makes a whistle in the Wally-wall-wall."

At night we slept stretched out on the seats. Dreaming of starting school in the fall with my old friends, I was startled to awaken among the faded plush seats with their stale smell of tobacco. I gradually remembered that we were moving to Colorado.

Part II.

Center and Boulder, Colorado, 1910-1918

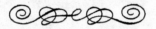

Chapter 17: Those First Busy Days

*T*he mountains burst on us like Judgment Day.

We called each other to come and see two tiny puffing engines pulling our train up La Veta Pass. At the top of the Pass the train stopped—to rest the engines, we supposed, just as Papa stopped a wagon at the top of a hill to rest the horses. Then we were rushed down the other side into the San Luis Valley, running smoothly to Monte Vista and Papa.

It was a joyful reunion at the depot. Welcoming us to our new home, Papa kissed us and said, "It's sure good to see you and the children, Mag." As our bedding, trunks, and suitcases were loaded into the wagon, he barraged us with questions as if he couldn't get enough answers, about Julia, the folks back home, how we liked the train ride. We started down the long Gunbarrel Road, which he said ran the full length of the Valley, the longest stretch of straight road anywhere around.

Mountains surrounded us. To the east the lofty Sangre de Cristo peaks were topped with snow, standing out like meringue on a lemon pie. Papa explained that Spanish explorers had named them "the blood of Christ" while viewing the range as it turned crimson at sunset. On the west was the Continental Divide, at the top of which, Papa said, the waters parted, some to flow east to the Atlantic Ocean, some west to the Pacific. "We're a mile-and-a-half high right now," Papa added, the Valley being 7,500 feet above sea level.

He flooded our minds with information.

The sky was a vivid blue, the air morning-fresh, the sun bright and warm even though ice formed on little puddles by the roadside. Water from an artesian well made a crystal fountain.

"Has the garden plot been plowed?" Mamma asked.

Papa took satisfaction in saying gardens were planted later here, where frost was known to come every month of the year.

We traveled twelve miles north on the Gunbarrel, then turned east to drive the two miles to Center, which was to be our town. Papa pointed out farms of people who would be our neighbors, the Deitrichs and Joneses, and then there was our house. It was low and cream-colored with a wide bay window, a white fence, and trees that looked small compared to our Missouri mulberries.

We did not stop but went on a quarter of a mile, crossed an irrigation ditch, and on to Uncle Frank and Aunt Jessie's. Uncle Frank, a favorite uncle, treated us just as if we were grownups. Aunt Jessie, his new wife, was tall and pretty with blue eyes and black hair. We ate dinner from their green flowery Haviland china with silverware that had heavy grapes embossed up and down the handles. The round table we ate on was oak, but the furniture in the parlor was shiny dark mahogany, and there was a piano in another small room. Flowered rugs almost covered the entire floor, a border of wood showing around them. They had a bathroom that opened off the kitchen, water supplied by an artesian well through the efforts of a busy little pump that put-putted noisily and importantly.

Papa had bought some furniture and Mamma began unpacking. She sent away to Sears, Roebuck for lace curtains to hang at the bay window and, when she had more time, began making braided and crocheted rugs and sent old carpets away to have them woven into new. She bought a little vacuum cleaner which had to be pumped by hand.

We too had an artesian well that kept a trough filled with fresh water for the horses, a delight of my father. It also provided water for the house and for irrigating the garden, which was one of Mamma's delights—water at any time without waiting for rain, rich sandy soil easy to cultivate, and sunshine every day for growing. Horses, cows, chickens, and white hogs (in Missouri they had been black) were soon part of the farm. The little pigs were cunning and sweet, their ears lined a delicate pink.

I especially remember the good suppers Mamma cooked quickly in those first busy days—fried potatoes, poached eggs, toast, and hot tea. Those were pleasant, exciting days of exploring the farm and discovering supple young willows along the irrigation ditches. At home we had woods and brooks; here we had open fields and ditches of cold mountain water. We were eager, trusting, and happy to be alive.

I had my first ride in an automobile, Uncle Frank's little red two-cylinder Cadillac. It looked like a buggy with no top and no doors (passengers stepped over the low sides into its one seat). It drove from the right-hand side, the driver reaching over the side to shift gears. As we whirled along at maybe fifteen to twenty miles an hour, we seemed to be going like the wind. I had fantasies of riding with a reckless young man at breakneck speed; I demanded he stop before both of us were killed.

Emerson said a gentleman never dodges. But it should be remembered that there were fewer things to dodge in Emerson's day. If modern gentlemen didn't dodge, they wouldn't be gentlemen very long. The excitement of the ride was of greater interest than the daydream, never brought to a denouement. There would be others. It took very little to set me off on a fantasy.

Chapter 18: Into the Mountains

*C*enter, with its low buildings and wide streets that needed no paving, was in the middle of the San Luis Valley. There lived the people who had created it—confident, energetic, full of pride and plans. It had the image of a town on its way, not one that had been there. It was young enough to have the brash assurance of the builder and old enough to have acquired leading citizens who felt they had it made. These couples would go to Denver, a city exhilarating in fresh-mined gold, always traveling on a Rio Grande Railroad pass. Anybody who was anybody at all could get one. They went to theaters and cafés and brought home furniture and rugs, china and silver, then regaled their neighbors with tales of frolicking in Denver.

At the intersection of the two business streets in Center stood a round water trough fed by an artesian well. Put a hole down almost anywhere in the valley and water would burst forth as it did when Moses smote the rock. A spectacular winter sight was the well frozen into a cascade of gleaming ice with water spouting above it.

On one corner stood the bank and next to it was the Center Mercantile Company, the only two-storied building in town. With the valley spreading around it, Center had no need to stack its buildings. The mercantile was a general store, food on one side, dry goods on the other; above it was the Center Opera House, reached by broad stairs from the sidewalk. It was a place for dances, school entertainments, lodge meetings, and an occasional road show. In it I saw my first play, a melodrama that sent me into shivers of delight and occupied my thoughts and fantasies for months. The stage curtain was a mountain scene. Tucked into the crags and crevices were ads of local merchants. (One was for my Uncle Frank's business, Carney and Bennington.)

About a quarter of the people of Center were Mexican-Americans, who lived on the east side in houses made mostly by themselves of sun-dried adobe. They attended a Catholic church in Del Norte, twelve miles away, since Center had only Methodist and Baptist churches. Many of them had come to work in the sugar beet fields, but beets did not turn out to be a profitable crop. Then it was learned that potatoes could bring that Midas touch to the area.

It was said that one crop of potatoes, sold on a good market, could pay for the land on which it grew. If a sudden freeze came early, before the potatoes were dug, however, the crop was a total loss. It was called a gambler's crop. No radio or television forecast the weather, but farmers learned to keep a wary eye for signs. Along in early September, when the frost was not far away, to dig or not to dig could be a heads or tails toss.

Whole Mexican families came to the fields to pick and sack the potatoes, making it a kind of holiday for them and the farmer's family. Young children played; older children worked. In addition to pay by the sack, the pickers got their potatoes for the winter. The sacks had to be hauled to the market, whatever the prevailing price was. In later years farmers built big cellars to store potatoes for future selling on a better market.

Papa was happy in Colorado. It had no mud, which he detested. The soil was light, sandy, and easily worked. And best of all, too little or too much rain was no worry. Melting snow flowed down from the mountains to water the crops.

Mamma merely accepted Colorado. If she was lonely, nobody knew it. Unlike my father, who talked to everybody he met and learned their religion, politics, and family statistics in a few minutes of conversation, she was taciturn with strangers. She looked after her house, garden, and chickens and applied her skills to her new home.

Wind blew every day, strong and steady, whipping balls of dried thistle along the roads until they lodged in fences. Mamma hated the wind as much as Papa had hated the mud, and she seemed to be fighting it constantly with her hoe. She set out strawberries, currants, and lush red raspberries that grew to perfection in that soil and climate. She experimented with head lettuce (later to be a big commercial crop), and her sweet peas bloomed faster than they could be picked.

Gnats and mosquitoes were pests. The gnats got in their licks during the warmth of the day; the mosquitoes at evening clanned gregariously around irrigation ditches. Papa wore a big red bandanna draped around his head under his hat for protection from gnats. I wore newspapers under my heavy cotton stockings for armor against mosquitoes. George didn't seem to mind either. He and the Deitrich twins, Robert and Robley, and their older brother John moved too fast for mere insects. He had a bicycle and rode it with the grace of a circus performer.

The mountains enchanted us. Mamma, who in Missouri would stop her work to listen to a meadowlark, loved to watch the shadows move across the hills and the sunsets flaming on the Sangre de Cristo range. Papa would come in some mornings and announce, "There's snow on Old Baldy."

We were eager to go to the mountains. In August Papa took us on a camping trip with two neighbor children, Mae and Danny Jones. We filled a wagon with a tent, hay and grain for the horses, coats and sweaters, fishing gear, dishes, bedding, tablecloths, and a considerable amount of food. At horse-pace, the mountains unfolded slowly, a prelude that mixed meadows and ranches with foothills and gave promise of grandeur to come. We were impatient to round each curve to see what lay beyond. The first night we stopped in a canyon beside a swift-moving stream. Papa and the boys drove stakes and put up the tent while the womenfolk unpacked the bedding and dishes and started supper. We peeled and fried potatoes, cooked ham, and made coffee over a fire built on the ground, then ate to the music of water tumbling over rocks with tall mountains standing by, pine trees making perpendiculars on their sloping sides. Mamma wished Julia was here.

After supper water carried from the creek was heated in a bucket for dishwashing. The food was put away, the beds made, and we walked about until daylight began drifting away. Papa said he wanted to stop sooner the next night, so he could catch fish for supper. Mamma said she wanted to pack the things better in the morning so they would be easier to get to. By lantern light we crawled into our beds.

When everybody was asleep I slipped out of the tent to see how the mountains looked at night. They had turned from green slopes to high dark walls that leaned over the stream. Only the flowing water broke the stillness and it seemed to be a part of it. I stood fearful and awestruck, then crept back into the tent and lay thinking of monstrous black mountains closing in on us.

In the morning, warmed by the breakfast of ham and eggs and coffee, we took down the tent, rolled it up, washed and packed the dishes, hitched up the horses, and were on our way, inching higher and higher along the canyon and across the meadows. At noon we snacked on ham sandwiches, cookies, and fruit. Later, when shadows began creeping up the mountainsides as they do so early in the hills, we made camp for the night.

The third night we camped where we were to stay for the rest of the trip and set up housekeeping. We began to feel we were experienced campers. Papa, as he did at home, cautioned us not to wander away and get lost and to be careful not to fall off a cliff. George and Danny leaped nimbly from rock to rock and went on exploring expeditions. Papa fished for trout and Mamma gathered wild flowers which she put in a glass for a table bouquet. Mae and I took off our shoes and stockings to wade in a little pool the creek had made and found it icy cold.

We climbed mountains that seemed the top of the world, but from each summit a higher peak beckoned. When it was attained, others rose beyond. One day Mamma, Mae, and I were stunned to reach the top of a peak and see before us a great valley far away, looking like a big blue lake bordered by the distant Sangre de Cristo range. The glory and exhilaration of the hills were a joy that grew and deepened as the days passed. Although we went to the mountains many more times in the years that followed, the ecstasy of that first trip with horse and wagon was never equaled.

Chapter 19: Flickerings

*N*o timber grew in our valley except for willows along irrigation ditches and trees that had been set out for ornament. In Missouri we had burned wood in our stoves. In Colorado people burned coal. To save money that would have been spent for coal, and, possibly, too, because Papa liked burning wood, he sometimes drove to the mountains with a team and wagon to gather chunks of rich, gnarled pine that were there for the taking.

By four o'clock in the morning he was up at the barn to feed and harness the horses while Mamma cooked a big breakfast and packed his lunch. George and I, attuned to the day, awakened at the sound of preparations and got up, not wanting to miss any part of the adventure. We offered ourselves as wood gatherers but were told we would "tire out" and Papa concluded that he wouldn't have time to look after us.

With the wagon loaded with axe, saw, and hatchet, Papa was ready to start long before daylight. We all went out to open the gate and see him off, Mamma urging him to be careful. As he went alone in the chill dark, we listened to the wagon wheels painfully grinding on the graveled road. The day was long with waiting. At evening we did the chores, ate supper, and in the soft dusk sat on the porch and listened.

Then would come, faint and far away, the sound of his

wagon wheels, and Mamma would go into the house to put more wood on the fire. There was a rejoicing of reunion as if his absence had been years long rather than a day as Papa turned in at the gate, guided by the lantern held as high as George could reach. Our Odysseus had returned to his Penelope and family. We shined the lantern on the wood he brought, chunks of pine from trees that once stood tall on the mountainsides. Sometimes there would be odd rocks he brought us. We questioned whether he had seen a deer; we wanted to hear about wild, unafraid animals and beavers making dams.

While Papa was eating and after the excitement had burned to a glow, Mamma would say she had been afraid he might have plunged over a cliff or cut himself with the axe and nobody would have known where to look for him. A load of wood from the mountains! How dull it made buying a ton of coal in town!

In Missouri neighbors came to help for a day and went home at night. In Colorado we had a "hired man" who lived in the house. In his poem "The Death of the Hired Man," Robert Frost gave him an image of pride—"He said he'd come to ditch the meadow"—but his true worth has not truly been acknowledged. The hired man came and went with the seasons and nobody asked whence or whither. He was likely to be middle-aged and have no connection with the community. He lived in his employer's house and ate at his table, but rarely had a room of his own or a place to keep his few belongings except in his suitcase under his bed. He accepted his place in the family as a matter of course, and the family accepted him.

Our "Shorty" Carver—he must have had a first name, but nobody used it—oozed self-confidence and concerned himself with what went on in our little town. He picked up more gossip than the sewing society and never tired of making jokes about the "Old Maid's Club," a name he gave to a group of unmarried working women. He had a native wit and in a different setting might have been a noted social commentator, both admired and feared.

Later, we hired Chris Hansen, a sturdy Scandinavian, young, good-looking, quiet mannered. He took his recreation at the pool hall and sometimes returned with a large box of candy he had won, which he promptly gave to me. This displeased Papa, whose attitude ruined my pleasure in the gifts. I was still fifteen.

How did a young farm worker drift into the condition of being a hired hand? For one reason or another he had not married, but he was not foot-loose and free like the tramp printer, the romantic vagabond of the road who showed up suddenly at a small newspaper office, worked a few days or weeks, and was off again. A hired man would stay as long as he was needed and the next year might turn up again and ask if there was any work.

I do not think these seasonal workers thought of themselves as unfortunate, as portrayed in Frost's poem: "nothing to look backward to with pride, / And nothing to look forward to with hope." They spoke often with pride of how they had stayed in the field to get the hay stacked before a rain came; they helped plan for the threshing and what should be planted on the back forty next year. They had a sense of proprietorship in the work they did and a feeling of independence in their coming and going.

In May of the second year we were in Colorado, Julia gave birth to a daughter, Edna Mabel, and came near losing her life. Mamma left immediately for Missouri and the rest of us waited anxiously for news. I prayed long and earnestly and made bargains with God. A few months later Julia visited Colorado with her baby and we were all happy. A son, Everett, had been born to Uncle Frank and Aunt Jessie at about the same time and it was a summer of admiring the two babies.

George and I entered school soon after we came to Colorado, he in the sixth grade, I in the eighth. George, with his quick speech, bright ways, and blond insouciance, was soon a favorite. He had minor brushes with teachers, but everybody knew he was there. I was also a leader in my class—of two students. George and I came from a one-room country school and here we were in a town school that had five rooms—two upstairs—and I was in one of them.

The school library had more books than I had ever seen, and I read constantly—stories by Horatio Alger and Jack London, romantic novels, poetry. Florence Deitrich became my best friend and we read books together, recommending favorites to each other. Her parents had eight children whose friends were welcomed for Sunday dinner—or any meal. There was always room for one more at their crowded table. After the dishes were washed on Sunday afternoons during the growing season, Adam and Carrie Deitrich walked out to inspect the crops, followed by their flock. Like her parents, Florence was warm and loving and laughing and I have never had a better friend.

I finished the grades that first spring, then started the two-year high school. I loved all the new studies. During the second year Mr. Hesler, the principal, made Julius Caesar come alive for me in three dimensions, all at the same time. In his literature class we read Shakespeare's *Julius Caesar*. In his ancient history class we studied the reign of Caesar. And in his second year Latin class we read Caesar's *Commentaries*. Mr. Hesler, in addition to being principal, taught four or five classes. In fact, he with one other teacher taught all the high school classes. His wife was a musician, who that year composed "The Sinking of the Titanic," one of those descriptive compositions, heavy bass when the ship hit the iceberg, solemn music when the lifeboats were launched.

And there were the flickerings of love. I had a crush on Willie Graham, a good-looking boy with wavy blond hair, who played piano and worked in the hotel, a large residence that had been converted into sleeping rooms. Mine was a secret crush. I wouldn't have dreamed of letting Willie know how much I liked him. Knowing where he hung his hat, the first thing I did when I got to school was look to see if his hat was there, which meant he was. But all the girls liked Willie and he liked them. Several of us would gather round to listen to him play the piano. He never showed any favoritism, liking to laugh and talk with all of us. In later years when I returned to Center to visit my parents, I would ask about Willie, but nobody ever seemed to know. These many years afterwards I think of Willie and Mr. Hesler, of how Florence and I giggled about a Roman named Galba in beginning Latin, who occupied a similar position in our text as Dick did in my children's first grade reader—"Run, Dick, run. See Dick run."

Forty years later, on a visit to my parents, I watched the W.P.A. cut down trees which as a child I had helped plant on Arbor Day. We had stood solemnly around the teacher singing "Arbor Day, O Arbor Day" to the tune of "Maryland, My Maryland" while the trees were set, water poured, and earth shoveled in. My emotions on that long-ago day were mingled. The quarter holiday gave the occasion the flavor of a picnic, but the serious words of the principal (whose hair standing straight up in front earned him the nickname of "Stubby") concerned our obligation to plant trees so that little children of the future might play under their branches. The ceremony smacked of church, and the fresh pile of earth was tinged with the mysterious sadness of a burial. "Stubby" has long passed on to his reward, and perhaps it is just as well that he did not know that a future generation, instead of being grateful for the shelter of the trees he set, chopped them down to plant Chinese elms.

On the last day of school after everybody had gone I went back alone and stood again in our room, looked at all the familiar things, and touched my desk in a sentimental farewell. Next year I would be graduated, in another school at another place. What was my future to be? What would happen to me in the years ahead?

Suddenly and for the only time in my life I had an overpowering sense of something that was to come, something mysterious and shadowy and unknown. Tears flowed down my face. The strange feeling took possession of me, sharp and troubling, and is vividly remembered.

I had come to a turning point. The two years of high school had ended and my parents were considering where to send me to finish. They chose the high school in the county seat town of Saguache, an Indian word meaning "blue water." It was a little town lying against the foothills in the north end of the valley. The principal, H. Clay Marks, drumming up business for the school, had come and talked to us. Papa asked, in the interest of economy, if I could take the last two years of high school in one. "She can try," he said.

Room and board were arranged with a family in Saguache and early in September I went away to school—and to my appointment with someone toward whom we had been moving all our lives. In later years I could not bear to think: What if my parents had sent me to Monte Vista or Del Norte?

Chapter 20: Falling in Love

"𝒯his is Mr. Greene, the science teacher and assistant principal." I do not remember who said these words to me halfway up the aisle of the Methodist Church in Saguache, Colorado, the Sunday before school opened, but I know that something happened to me when I looked into the deep-set, dark brown eyes of Milton Willard Greene. It must have happened to him, too. In a few weeks we were "going together."

I was seventeen and that was the beginning of the most marvelous year of my life. Love came and I was flooded with a secret radiance that heightened every perception. That love gave me the strength of ten and filled me with an inward power and glory. Everything I did seemed touched by magic.

The principal of the school, H. Clay Marks, was two years out of the University of Kansas, and Mr. Greene was two years out of Wooster College in Ohio. It was, for both of them, their second year at Saguache High School. A fluttery, throaty, spinsterish woman taught English and was bedeviled by rowdiness in her classes. On Saturdays she often invited me to her barn-like house for tea and cookies, more likely tea and sympathy.

The fourth teacher was a brisk, efficient woman who taught elocution. It was a time when people spoke pieces. She coached plays and guided each student through a reading to be performed before an audience. It was a special kind of teaching and Saguache had it only because the woman's husband had moved there in his business.

The schoolhouse was a modest two-story brick, just the right size for the forty to fifty students enrolled. The basketball court was on the grounds, and Mr. Greene was the coach, as well as the track coach. (He had been a runner at Wooster.) The school had no football team.

In his classes I studied physics, chemistry, algebra, and geometry. My other classes were American history, English and American literature, Vergil, and Cicero. I studied Cicero after school with Mr. Marks in order to complete my two years' work in one.

In everything I yearned for perfection; nothing less was good enough. Though I had always been studious and bookish, I now had the joyful incentive of pleasing a teacher I loved. Grades in the high nineties were sent home to my parents with such comments as "Splendid work" and "A superior student" written across the cards by Mr. Marks. I have never studied so well or learned so much as I did in that year. If I had not fallen in love or had fallen in love with somebody else besides a teacher, might I have mooned away the evenings and dropped into the low nineties?

The first day in the Vergil class Mr. Marks's emphasis on the meter of the *Aeneid* gave me the impression that we were expected to render it into English iambic pentameter. I labored over it long into the night and produced some fairly passable verse, but was greatly relieved to learn that a prose translation was sufficient.

A student "keeping company" with a teacher in a small town attracts comment, particularly when Mr. Greene and I double-dated (though that term had not yet been coined) with Mr. Marks and Effie Scovil, a special student in Mr. Greene's German class. The four of us played chess. We took walks on Sunday afternoons into the nearby hills, skipped stones on a little pond, and, when the sun neared the distant purple mountains, walked slowly back to town. They were the most beautiful walks I have ever taken in all my life and if

Mr. Greene touched my arm to assist me, stars were lighted.

The four of us sang in the Methodist choir, which rehearsed on Thursday evenings. How we made "Men of Harlech" ring out and what vigor we put into the "Hallelujah Chorus"! Mr. Greene had a fine tenor voice, many remarked. We labored over the Christmas and Easter music and had something good for every Sunday. I have never sung so well in all my life as I did that year.

Saguache was dominated subtly but definitely by a group of close-knit old families, and nobody can be more clannish than old families in a small town where it becomes habit more than intent to associate chiefly with each other. The town had two banks, a hotel (Mr. Marks and Mr. Greene lived in the hotel and complained wittily about it), a garage that offered day or night livery service, and a millinery store that advertised "hats made to your individual order."

Now and then there was a picture show—motion pictures were just beginning—but we did not go to any except one at the end of the year. I remember, too, that a hypnotist came to town and a woman lay in a trance in a store window all day, attracting curious, questioning, and embarrassed looks. Various other events entertained the townspeople—horse races in the dust roads outside of town, fights and wrestling matches—and there was hushed talk of cockfights.

We attended none of these, but something we did frequent were the Lyceum lectures, for which season tickets were sold. Mr. Greene began asking me to go with him and we both tacitly understood that we would continue to go together. Some boys at school, hoping to "get ahead of the professor," hatched up the plan for one of them to ask me to the next lecture. Charles Scovil, a nice-looking boy, Effie's brother, was chosen for the assignment. He stopped me one day after class and made his pitch. I did not hesitate nor did I feel coy. Straightforwardly I said, "I always go with Mr. Greene."

On the day before a lecture, a bully and troublemaker created a disciplinary problem and struck Mr. Greene, giving him a black eye. It caused a big stir and the boy was immediately expelled. He belonged to a prominent family and his sister was one of my best friends. Mr. Greene suggested that, considering his appearance, it might be better if we did not go to the lecture together. I said I would like to go with him as planned and that is what we did. Although I do not recall the name of a single lecture, I am certain that I have never enjoyed going to lectures as greatly as I did that year.

I do not remember being at all concerned about my looks or clothes. My dresses, made by Mamma, were few and simple and I had no cosmetics of any kind, but at seventeen who needs them? Pictures in the school annual show me with a lumpy pompadour and a white blouse with a jumper I remember as a rose-colored tussah. The little gold star I wore over my heart was for perfect attendance at Sunday School for a year—or was it five? Once when we were in the mountains, I went to Sunday School at Creede to keep my record for perfect attendance.

Neita Fleming, a bright girl with really gold hair and blue eyes, and I were on a debate team that won what was described as a "magnificent silver loving cup" to have and to hold for one year. We took the negative of the topic: "Resolved, that the railroads of the nation should be owned and operated by the Federal government." It was the year I did the best debating of my life. I had not debated before—and have not since.

Mr. Greene taught me more than science and math. He taught me to play chess and tennis, and, helping with the debate, corrected my Missouri hills dialect. I was surprised and embarrassed when he said I pronounced the word "there" as though it was spelled "thar." I cannot remember what we talked about besides school and self-improvement when we were together, but it was not about love.

I watched him at the blackboard explaining a geometry theorem, saw him on the grounds coaching sports, and loved every sight and sound. When I did geometry problems at night I used his initials, MWG, Milton Willard Greene, to designate angles. I was not on his girls' basketball team, but

Neita was a forward and a whiz. I wrote an essay for a D. A. R. contest on the subject "The Triumph over Mars," in which I proved that there would never be another war and won honorable mention. (That was one year before the First World War broke out.) One day the entire student body—except guess who—went AWOL. I did not feel virtuous or smug for staying, but embarrassed and ill at ease sitting there all by myself, but, with my upbringing, skipping school was something I could not do.

For graduation exercises Mamma made me two new dresses—a blue dress for the baccalaureate sermon and a pretty white dress of soft, silky material with narrow lace whipped to tucks around the skirt. Although my grades qualified me, I was not the valedictorian, not having gone to the school the entire four years. That went to Neita, a well-deserved honor. Nine of us were graduated in that class of 1913.

Mr. Greene and Mr. Marks obtained a scholarship for me to Colorado State University and persuaded my parents to let me have a go at education there instead of at the state normal, where Papa proposed sending me, thinking of a teaching certificate. I had already taken the county examinations and obtained a certificate, for I was to teach in a country school two miles north of Center that fall, a school that was part of the Center school district.

The next year Mr. Greene went to Tarpon Springs, Florida, where he became superintendent of schools, and Mr. Marks to Deland, Florida. At the end of the graduation program something occurred that startled the drowsy audience awake. Mr. Marks said something about the attitude of the town toward the school and most of it was not complimentary.

After the close of school Mr. Greene came to Center for a short visit with my parents before he went to Kansas, the home of his parents. I think Mamma, Papa, and Uncle Frank had a feeling that a slick young teacher from back East who took an interest in a backward country girl was up to no good, but I was happy to have him in the house talking to

Papa about farming and asking Mamma about Missouri. No girl brought home a beau with greater pride.

Looking back, I can smile at that girl, so artless and undesigning, accepting loving without question. There is a wistfulness, too, for her wholeness, her freshness of youth uncorroded by time—and pain, at the memory of the years that are gone.

Thinking back over the year I would tell myself, "He'll ask me some day."

He had not so much as touched me except to take my arm as we walked home from choir practice or the Lyceum. Walking along in the dark, his arm through mine, I wanted it never to end. No word of love passed his lips, yet I felt as sure of it as though a ring was on my finger.

Standing in the bay window of our little house with dark sifting down and the mountains a deep blue shadow, he kissed me and in that kiss promises were silently made. I had become eighteen and nothing, I knew, would ever be as glorious as that year of falling in love, and it never has been.

Chapter 21: Lessons

From my earliest years I thought of myself as a schoolteacher. Three months out of high school, I was teaching in a country school, North Center. After years of playing school, I took to teaching like a bird to air.

I stayed at home with my parents and walked two miles to school every day—except when the weather was cold or stormy. Then I rode a horse. (A photograph of 1918 shows me mounted—wearing a sturdy velvet hood and a long, divided riding skirt pulled over my dress, all made by my mother. The impression is that of a penitent setting forth on a pilgrimage.) My pay was fifty dollars each month and my duties, in addition to teaching, included sweeping and cleaning the schoolroom and keeping the fire going when the weather got cold.

My twelve scholars ranged over four grades. I have warm memories of Rachael, a bright, shy, small girl in the first grade who spoke in a low voice. In her dark dresses coming almost to her shoe tops, she had an elfin look that drew me to her. Two boys larger than I were only a few years younger. They vied to feed and water my horse at noon and bring in wood and water before school. They would raise their hands and ask permission to put a stick of wood in the stove.

The day always opened with the Lord's Prayer—Madalyn Murray O'Hair had not yet spoken out—and nobody came to help or hinder, except the county superintendent on an annual inspection visit. The children and I were out in the country on our own and we began to love each other. Soon parents spoke of the progress being made by their children, particularly the mother of two sisters in the first grade, Alice and Esther Morris. This year of teaching was a happy experience, natural and good. The children learned and I learned.

Summer came and ahead of me was the thrill of going to the University of Colorado in Boulder. A Saguache girl who would be a senior that year, Louise Woodard, arranged for me to live where she did with a Mr. and Mrs. Clemmer, an elderly couple who kept a few women roomers in their home. Louise said I would need a gym suit and Mamma made me one, a navy middy blouse and bloomers.

Other sewing was done; two cotton dresses, a black and white print with diagonal ruffles that I basted and stitched, ripped and sewed, and ripped again and dampened the seams with sweat and tears, learning that she who sews must also rip. I had a blue checked cotton dress trimmed with white embroidery and a tan dress, worn with long dangling beads of tiny pine cones.

With this wardrobe and a few other things I took a night train to Denver on a railroad pass, paying an additional two dollars for a Pullman berth, my first experience, and from Denver took an interurban train to Boulder. When I heard the University station announced I got off, not knowing that the person who was to meet me, our neighbor, Neal Jones, was waiting for me at the depot downtown.

Enough blunders were made that year to last a lifetime, but they rolled off quickly and were forgotten. Nothing could dampen my joy; I was in college! I had never been on a college campus and knew nothing about life at a university. When asked if I had a Big Sister, an upperclasswoman assigned to a freshman to help her get started, I said, thinking of petite Julia, "I've got an older sister, but she isn't very big." At a large dinner for new students I was shocked when songs were sung—right at the table. One of Papa's absolute rules was no singing at the table.

The Clemmers lived next door to the Pi Beta Phi house and I wondered at the number of girls rooming there. They seemed more than the house would hold. I knew nothing about sororities and fraternities, but was soon hearing talk of rush parties and who was being pledged. Though the weather was still warm, many girls took to wearing wool suits. It was rumored that one sorority was pledging only girls with fur trim on wool suits.

One thing I did know, however, was how to study and I did well. One of my favorite classes was beginning German, my first venture into a modern language—Mr. Greene's influence. It was taught by Herr Bauer, a native German, who would read "Du bist wie eine Blume" with swimming eyes and a faraway sadness on his face. Was he seeing some beloved young girl he once knew?

One day he was late to class. The students began talking about his funny ways. In one of my brash moods, I imitated his speech and was applauded with such loud laughter that no one noticed when Herr Bauer entered the room until he purred smoothly, "Miss Bennington seems so competent that perhaps she would like to take over the class for today?" And that is what I did and didn't really mind doing at all. An early symptom of independence is brashness.

I studied every evening, still wanting nothing less than perfection. A teacher in advanced composition, a big, raw-boned man, led us into the deep waters of linguistic semantics. He liked to discuss a theory he had: that farmers would be less lonely if they lived together in a village with their land extending out from the center like pieces of pie. (That theory was the blueprint of a New England vegetarian group planning to go to territorial Kansas. It failed before it had a chance to succeed because the organizers sent ahead to lay out the land and make preparations had not done their homework.) In his large lecture course on Western Europe I learned his personal views about the arrogance of kings and popes. His emphasis on the sale of papal indulgences was a bit stronger than might be expected from an impartial professor.

In an analytical geometry class I learned about curves that stretched off into infinity and yet could be charted by symbols on paper. The teacher, a tall, slender woman with the imagination of a poet, had the gift of making parabolas sing. She talked to me about majoring in mathematics.

The director of women's physical education was a Miss Bunting, a small, trim (but not prim) woman from an eastern college. Students exercised in two long rows, executing her orders snapped out like a drill sergeant's. Nothing excused a girl from gym except illness or menstruation, and Miss Bunting was dogmatic about the difference between the two. "Menstruation," she said, speaking the word right out loud in class to the embarrassment of many, was not an illness, and at such times the excuse should be marked "M," not "sick."

One day Miss Bunting, stopping a vigorous class drill, asked me to step forward. "Don't you have a white blouse?" she asked. (While all the other students wore white tops with dark bloomers, it had not bothered me at all that I alone wore a navy middy.) I said I did not. "Can you get one?" she demanded. That afternoon I bought a commercially made white middy blouse and for the first time felt conspicuous and self-conscious in her class.

Miss Bunting's May Fete, an annual event, was straight out of Sherwood Forest with Robin Hood and Maid Marian, the latter making a grand entrance astride a horse. A senior who excelled in sports was chosen as Marian, but she had no mount. Another girl promptly volunteered her horse, one she declared was not safe for anybody else to ride. She was then awarded the role of Marian. As one of her maids of honor, I danced on the green in a long yellow gown with flowers in my hair. (Another gym class activity on the green, not connected with the May Fete, was performed on the quadrangle, marked off with small squares. In each square was a slip of paper containing the name of a student who was expected to rid that spot of dandelions.)

My first brush with psychology came in a class taught by a Dr. Cole, a teacher reported to have "advanced ideas." Some said he didn't believe in the Bible. Parents at the time worried their children would come home from college questioning sound doctrine. Some years later they worried that children would come home believing in communism. I loved the psychology class, admired Dr. Cole, and felt honored when he walked a distance with me after classes and asked about my home and family.

Everybody said I mustn't miss Dean Bigelow's course in early English literature. Miss Antoinette Bigelow, the handsome, full-figured, middle-aged dean of women, taught only that one class. With rapturous face she would read from Malory's *Le Morte d'Arthur*, lingering over the love of Guinevere and Launcelot. She loved *Beowulf*—and all young heroes—and was touched by poems of unrequited love. It was an echo of my own romantic feelings about poetry and the class should have been perfect, but something went wrong.

Although I loved poetry, I had never been introduced to breaking it down for scansion, rhetoric, and academic interpretation. I knew I was not doing well, but did not know why. One day I took my book out on the campus, sat against a tree to study, but could not see the words for tears. Near the end of the semester Dean Bigelow called me into her office to talk about my work. "I feel I ought to fail you," she said, "but you have an A in all your other classes. What went wrong here?" Holding back tears, I tried to tell her. She gave me a passing grade.

My other poor grade was in biology, where the dissecting of earthworms and crayfish was even more distressing than dissecting poems into trochees and recessive accents. Nevertheless, during my second year I was invited to a meeting of the Phi Beta Kappa Society as a likely candidate and was elected to a junior honor society, Hesperia. Invited to join a sorority, I declined.

Drama and journalism were extracurricular, with no

credit given. I was in several plays and became a reporter for the *Silver and Gold*, the school newspaper. At a meeting called to get volunteer reporters, I wanted to speak up, but was in one of my timid spells. John McCann, sitting beside me, whispered, "Go on. You can do it." So I became a reporter and have spent most of my life on a newspaper. John McCann, a law student from the East, was thoughtful, generous, kind, intelligent, and gentle, and, as if these attributes were not enough, he was quite good-looking. He was Louise Woodard's beau and perhaps for that reason he was always kind to her freshman friend.

Generally speaking, the girls at the University were of two sorts—those mainly interested in social life and those chiefly interested in education, but they overlapped at times. Dating was an important campus activity—it was called *fussing*, known at various other times as *sparking*, *petting*, *necking*, or *smooching*, and I'm sure was and is just as pleasant under one name as any other. I had a few beaus, not serious because of Mr. Greene, but I must confess that I did fall in love with the editor of the *Silver and Gold*, a tall, sandy-haired senior, a love that was secret and one-sided. I lost him, if you can lose something you have never had, to a Pi Phi with braces on her teeth. With a sigh for the ruthlessness of time, I must also confess I do not remember his name.

The library was a popular and lively place, except maybe on Wednesday evenings, when regular dates could be had. Of course, it was not so jolly on the main floor under the severe eye of the old lady of twenty-eight who checked out books. But down in the basement there was no eagle eye to reproach, and a happy pair could study together unmolested behind forty-six heavy volumes of the *Stories of the Operas*. All the magazines in the world, from the *Eden Enterprise* down, were there, bound in large volumes and stacked around to form cozy nooks. The dull phrases of a dead language fell into musty decay before the living words in the mouths of youth, and the study of *lepidoptera* could not compete with that of *homo sapiens*. Truly the greatest study of mankind is man.

School routine included chapel, held once a week in the unfinished auditorium of the new McKay building. Students who did not attend were asked to explain their absence. Equally well attended, although not compulsory, were rallies held around bonfires to whip up spirit for a big football game. As the players were introduced, we applauded and sang "Glory, glory, Colorado" to the tune of "The Battle Hymn of the Republic," waving our lacy handkerchiefs. The first line was "Folsom's eleven comes a-marching on the field" (Folsom was the coach). The games were played on a grassy place in front of wooden bleachers, and after a victory, freshmen pulled the rope of the tower bell at Old Main far into the night, often to the annoyance of the older residents of Boulder.

The University had strict rules for women students and my landlady, Mrs. Clemmer, although presiding over a private home, enforced them to the last dot, along with some of her own. Girls had to be in by ten except for weekend dances, and no dates were permitted during the week except on Wednesday evenings. Escorts waited in the hall for their dates to come downstairs. Need I say there was no cohabitating or coed rooming houses? Our landlady did not shut an eye until all her girls were safely locked inside the house.

One day I disregarded the rule of no laundry in the rooms and washed a pair of stockings. Somehow one fell through a hole in the closet floor over her pantry. Mrs. Clemmer brought the damp piece of hosiery to me with a cool question, "Is this yours?"

On Saturday mornings she called out that Mr. Clemmer was coming upstairs for his weekly bath and we should remain in our rooms with closed doors. Sometimes she would invite us into her parlor to listen to operatic records on the Victrola. She liked motion pictures and now and then would invite me to go with her to see Mary Pickford, Marguerite Clark, Douglas Fairbanks, or Theda Bara. She sat in the dark chuckling to herself, commenting to no one in particular in an undertone.

We seldom saw Mr. Clemmer, but had it from his wife that he would not go to the movies with her, thought them disgusting, and spent most of his time reading. She found many opportunities for reminding us that Mr. Clemmer had been graduated from Harvard and that her four brothers were graduates of Yale. She said nothing about how they happened to land in Boulder.

That year taught me a valuable lesson for life. Mrs. Clemmer was a sort of center for the distribution of "news." She passed on various items and opinions to and about her roomers. She told me that one of them—mentioning her name—had, it was said, a "pretty wild" reputation in her hometown. I did not translate that information into anything particularly derogatory. At home, girls who tore around on horses and helped drive cattle instead of helping their mothers in the house were so described. Then in one of our upstairs sessions when we were all trying to out-complain each other about the service in the house, I blurted out what she had said. The girl did not take "pretty wild" as tamely as I had and went to Mrs. Clemmer to demand what she had meant. I had not said anything that was not true. My fault was in saying it. Mrs. Clemmer never referred to the incident, but she gave me the iceberg treatment for the rest of the year, addressed me only when necessary and then by my last name only. These many years afterwards I can report that I am the soul of discretion, that I can be trusted with secrets and sorrows, both from friends and from people I write about in my newspaper column, and that I never betray a trust.

The University deepened, widened, and heightened my world and I loved it. I loved my classes, loved talking to teachers, loved the friends I made, and the good times. I especially loved "beefsteak fries." Boys brought the beefsteak and girls the rest of the food. We hiked into the nearby mountains, made a fire, cooked, ate, and sang. Then, when the fire had died down and been safely put out, we strolled slowly back down the canyon, often by moonlight.

Mr. Greene and I wrote each other often and he came up

from Florida to see me during a spring vacation. My father visited once and I took him about the campus, proudly introducing him to Dean Bigelow. In one of the classrooms he was shocked at the nudity of the casts of Greek statues and asked incredulously, "Do mixed classes meet here?"

Since popular fare drew students to Greenman's Restaurant, I took Papa there for a noonday meal of olive-nut sandwiches (the hamburger had not yet arrived in Boulder) and to listen to the sensuous, recorded music of Hawaiian guitars. He found both too exotic to his taste and wondered about his daughter's.

In style were the hobble skirt and the slit skirt, the latter long and straight, with a modest slit at each side, not only to reveal a seductive glimpse of shoe tops but to show a flash of colored petticoat. The layers of petticoats by this time had shrunk to one and had taken on rainbow hues, at least in the flounce. A button or two of the blouse was left casually unbuttoned, and sometimes a hint of curve could be seen. After I returned home to Center at the end of the term, I at once displayed my acquaintance with *haute couture* by leaving a bit of blouse unbuttoned. My father spoke up: "You forgot to button your blouse." I hastily buttoned up and said nothing.

Caresse Crosby had not yet invented the bra. Worn next to our skin was a garment called a vest, but it was really just a plain, white, knitted, cotton shirt, sleeveless and cut low. Over this went the corset, high enough to do service as a bra, but if a girl was full-bosomed, she wore a fitted corset cover. Next was the camisole, beribboned and lace-trimmed, then drawers, petticoat, and stockings, a good grade of black knitted cotton called lisle. Quality was not important since stockings were hidden by high shoes and long skirts.

Skirts started their upward mobility and in a year went all the way from ankle to shoe tops. With skirts hemmed up and swinging, we felt new and free and worldly, which is probably the way girls felt in later years when the mini skirt burst into style.

Loose powder was our only cosmetic. For evening allure, a beauty patch (a tiny black circle, square, crescent, or triangle) called attention to a rounded cheek or a high cheekbone. Veils were a daytime allure. Hair was swirled into a flat dip over the forehead and for a smooth look pulled to the back in a chignon. Bobbed hair was yet years in the future.

Girls sometimes borrowed each other's clothes for a special date. When I bought a new black plush velour coat, one of the girls in our house expressed disappointment that I had not chosen black velvet, which she said was preferred for evenings. Girls returned from evening dates and sat up late talking over everything that had happened. (It was always asked whether he opened his mouth when he kissed.) I learned at those midnight meetings many useful things not taught in classes.

Chapter 22: A Sweet, Singing Hour

or financial reasons, I did not go back to the University for a third year, but taught in the Center School. I quickly learned that children in the fifth and sixth grades have arrived at a felicitous place on the road to an education. They have progressed beyond the basics and have acquired an interest in reading, but are still young enough to be eager and curious, natural and free. They are not yet tainted with any symptom of the painful, early sophistication that attacks the teens. I loved them and loved teaching.

Among the Mexican children was Allie Pacheco, a bright but timid boy who bloomed through the year. Pat Deitrich, the youngest of the Deitrich family, our neighbors, was a bright boy with a sweet round face and bright blue eyes. And there was Minnie, who did not learn fast, but was gentle and loving. A solemn tow-headed boy named Theodore was not the quickest in the class, but he had a native perception that often bypassed the text. When his class was having a hard time with predicate nominatives, Theodore was the one who always had the right answers.

One day I said, "Theodore, can you tell us how you learned about predicate nominatives so quickly?"

His slow and earnest answer was totally honest: "I just say it the way it sounds awkwardest," which is a good description of that unpopular part of speech.

I read to the children every morning from books such as *White Fang* and *The Call of the Wild* and the Ernest Thompson Seton books. My students were interested in animals, people, and things, but not romance.

Several of us went to a state teachers' meeting in Pueblo, where I gave a paper on the teaching of reading and came home with a dress that caused my mother to shake her head in disbelief. I had paid *thirty-five dollars* for a navy silk dress with small box pleats held in by a wide embroidered cerise sash. Another extravagance was an apple green suit—*forty dollars!*—with apple green silk stockings to go with it. That was before either rayon or nylon stockings.

The real excitement in school was over a new young high school teacher, Ivor Simpson Roberts, whom we called *Kero*. He would play the piano in my room with a verve that drew children in from the playground to listen to "Pretty Baby" and "By the Light of the Silvery Moon." He could make a piano sound like a whole band. As soon as he walked into the building, a crowd began to gather.

Kero and I made a foursome with Zoa Ray, the primary teacher, and Pat, a depot agent. Under Kero's tutelage we learned a few chords on the ukulele, and we were soon singing about sweet brown maidens giving language lessons on Waikiki beaches. We managed church socials, strung popcorn and cranberries for the Christmas tree, made divinity fudge, and laughed about a woman who concerned herself to the principal about schoolteachers who were "keeping company." We laughed because we were young and happy.

Kero told us about his sister, Elizabeth Madox Roberts, author of *The Great Meadow* and other books about Kentucky and the frontier, and about his sister Lill in Colorado Springs. Once when we were in the mountains he recited something Elizabeth had written:

> Happy heart coming home from the far, far hills—
> How the primrose flamed in the Arctic chills,
> And you heard the flutes of the summit birds.
> You will keep forever their sky-lost words,

Happy heart, coming home from the hills.

Years later, while rummaging in an old box, I came across a bunch of spangled banding which revived memories of Kero. It had embellished a Grecian evening gown at a time in my life when the whole future seemed to hang on the slender bands of that classic creation.

For I had fallen in love with Kero and my soul burned with a single idea—that a Grecian evening gown was the one thing needed for a happy continuance of life. My dressmaker tactfully tried to persuade me to choose a more conservative model. But what did a middle-aged dressmaker know about love? I know now that my beauty was not the pure, classic, Helen-of-Troy type to carry off a Grecian evening gown, but at that time I thought I looked very well in it—and, more importantly, so did Kero.

The time came when I realized my dressmaker had been right. A Grecian evening gown was not quite the thing to wear to an Epworth League social or a box supper at District No. 7. But I was not sorry. I had had my moment—a sweet, singing hour of ecstasy set like a priceless jewel in the plain band of life.

At the end of the year Kero left for Kentucky, where he had a job the coming year, and we all went down to the depot to see him off. Kissing was not a casual, meaningless salute, but was given and received with feeling. There at the train, for the first and last time, he kissed me.

Chapter 23: Mrs. M. Willard Greene

*W*illard and I—it was no longer Mr. Greene—
were married on June 26, in my parents'
home with a few friends and neighbors
present and no attendants. Willard had a new navy
blue suit that was his "best" for years afterward. My white
georgette crepe dress from Franklin Simon in New York had
a tiered skirt and a square-necked blouse. I wore a white
georgette hat made over a wide wire frame and trimmed with
a few flowers. A friend sang two songs, "I Love You Truly"
and "O Promise Me." My mother made the wedding cake
with rice flour—for it was 1918. There was a war and wheat
was a scarce commodity.

Willard came a couple of days before the wedding,
bringing a bridal bouquet of lilies of the valley which I kept
under my bed and looked at every few hours, as though by
willing I could keep it fresh. Colorado weather was cool and
we had no refrigerator.

No photographs were taken and I have no newspaper
clippings. Gifts included a set of Community plate silver
(Adam pattern), cut glass, china, and other pieces. My pupils
at school brought me orange wrappers, which I sent away
with a small amount of money for a set of orange blossom
silverware. Mindful of the Missouri bridal dowry, my father
gave Willard a hundred dollars and said he should buy a
mattress. The club of unmarried women, called locally the

Old Maids Club, followed its custom of giving a dozen salad forks, utensils not in common family use and a hopeful step forward toward the niceties of living.

My trousseau was not elaborate. I had my apple green suit and my navy-cerise dress, a green and gold striped silk shirt, and white silk stockings that had green clocks. And I had my Grecian dress, a romantic indulgence, worn only that enchanted once with Kero. It was a pale pink crepe de Chine with flowing sleeves and a bodice confined with long bands of beaded crystal that crossed in front, then went to the back and returned to fall in a looped tie.

Why did I take it? What I would do with a Grecian dress in Center, Colorado, was not clear to my sensible mother and is not at all clear to me now. Nor is it at all clear what I did with it in the little cattle town of Bazaar, Kansas, where we were to move. Later I ripped it up, dyed it a brighter pink and converted it into an only slightly more appropriate dress with wide bands of blue embroidery, copying a dress I had seen in a magazine.

My shoes were high-topped, white, laced kid with a curving heel. They met the skirt halfway up the lower leg over stockings supposed to match the color of the dress. The favored undergarment was the all-in-one "teddy bear" or "ted." I made several, the most elaborate being of a violet print trimmed in lace. My special nightgown was a long white nainsook, Sears' best grade, attached to a wide crocheted lace yoke.

We were married simply and after the ice cream and cake we prepared to go to Wagonwheel Gap in the mountains for a short stay. Uncle Frank and Aunt Jessie were to drive us and we would return by train. We lingered, but when it came time to say goodbye I found my father out in the yard. "Now you take care, Hon," he said, "and write to us."

Uncle Frank and Aunt Jessie spent the night at the Gap in another cabin at a discreet distance. They were the ones who nine months later became the parents of a daughter. It was the earnest hope of brides to keep from becoming pregnant for at least a year, and they exchanged what meager and unreliable information they had.

At the Gap we swam in the pool, walked in the mountains, ate at the lodge, and began our new relationship as husband and wife. It seemed strange to be called by my new name, though I had said it many times to myself and had ordered calling cards imprinted with *Mrs. M. Willard Greene.* What need I would have for calling cards does not now come to mind.

We returned, packed the wedding gifts, visited another day or two, and left for Kansas on a train, taking a Pullman since we would be traveling overnight. Morning found us in Garden City, Kansas, where we got off the train to have breakfast at the Harvey House and transferred from the Pullman car to the day coach. A Pullman was for sleeping. The night was over.

art III.

Chase County, Kansas, 1918-1933

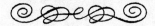

Chapter 24: The Flint Hills

*W*illard's parents met us in Strong City, the nearest town on the Santa Fe Railroad to their farm in Chase County, Kansas. I was filled with the anticipation and hesitation one feels when entering the unknown.

I barely knew my in-laws. I had visited the Greenes briefly one Christmas and had met Willard's brothers, Dwight and Churchill. (His married sisters I would not meet until after the war.) One summer Willard had driven his mother to Colorado for a short vacation. His father said she needed a rest, but I thought it likely, too, that she wanted to look over the Benningtons.

Talk on the way to the farm was quiet answers to my unending stream of questions. About a mile from Strong City and across the river was the town of Cottonwood Falls, which had a waterfall and an old mill used in early days to grind grain. Although they were called twin cities, they were competitive siblings. Strong City had won the depot; Cottonwood Falls the county courthouse, which stood high at the end of Main Street. It was a picture-perfect old limestone edifice built in the Renaissance style. Looming into view, the 1873 structure was as surprising and pleasing as if we had rounded a bend in the river and come upon an unexpected castle. Its elegance dominated the business buildings, a testament to someone's love of beauty.

My in-laws took a genuine pleasure in telling me about the family. Before long I learned that the first of the family in this country was Surgeon John Greene, who, with his wife, Joan Tattersall, sailed from Southampton, England, April 6, 1635. They arrived in Boston on June 2, after fifty-eight days on a sailing ship. Further back was Alexander, the great-grandson of one of the Norman nobles who had invaded England in 1066 with William the Conqueror.

Willard's mother, Virginia Moore, had given birth to nine children during her first nineteen years of marriage. All lived but the first, Fred, whose picture is on the dial of a watch still in the family. Many were the stories about her father, William Moore of Portsmouth, Ohio, whose ships, the steamer *Home*, and later the *Hope*, plied the Ohio and Mississippi Rivers to New Orleans and back. On these trips he often took his family, and it was on such an excursion in 1853 that my future mother-in-law was born while they were stopping over at Yazoo City, Mississippi.

The Civil War found them again in Mississippi, where they were detained by the Confederacy. Captain Moore, never in sympathy with the South, could not leave when the war began, so he continued running his boat until the Confederates "pressed it into the service." Suspected of being a Northern sympathizer, he exercised great caution. Being ordinarily a man of few words, he was now even more careful. On two occasions he took a company of Confederate soldiers to Vicksburg free of charge, which earned him what became the prize family heirloom, a large coin-silver pitcher, inscribed: "To Capt. William Moore from the Hamer Rifles." They presented him upon another occasion a gold-headed, rosewood cane inscribed, "Presented to Capt. William Moore by the Sartartia Rifles, May 13, 1861." Since the pitcher and cane could testify against Captain Moore when the Union Army finally took over Vicksburg, they were hidden from sight. There was also china from the *Hope*. It was rumored that in her senile years one of his daughters would wander about town handing out pieces of the set to anyone she met.

William Moore, a great reader, had a large library that included the elephant-folios of Audubon. Every creature, he claimed, had a right to live and he would kill none, not even a housefly, which he would liberate outside. Described as tall and solemn looking in a dark suit, usually a Price Albert with a silk hat, he was a dignified figure. Grandchildren were awed in his presence. When he was old and ill, the grandchild destined to become my husband was brought to visit and found him lying in a tall four-poster bed. The conversation was meager and halting, but the boy remembered a startling bit of advice given him that day: "Willie, always be careful about choosing your friends. I never met anyone I thought was worth having for a friend, so I never had any."

I was told about Mother Greene's sister, Aunt Louisiana Richter, whose sons were all doing well. Then there was Aunt Macey, a spinster sister, who enjoyed visiting cemeteries and could with little prompting recite dates and causes of death and supply endless details of final illnesses. I heard about Cousin Will Moore, who was doing well in Washington and who in later years corresponded with Willard.

Willard, whose full name was Milton Willard Greene, I learned was named for Frances E. Willard, the famous temperance leader, and for his mother's brother, Milton Moore, the father of the poet Marianne Moore. Willard had a natural lively wit which punctuated his mother's lengthy recitatives of family history. The only time I saw it fail him was on the next April Fool's Day. Still young enough to enjoy April Fool's pranks, on the last night of March I hid all his BVDs except one, which I adorned lavishly with lace and pink ribbons. Willard—a strong, silent man who would prefer a leopard skin to lavender shorts—gave voice to the blood-curdling cry of a wounded bull ape and went to work shivering through the chill April air.

Willard's father was the third Elisha Barton Greene. Two deep concerns had brought him from Zanesville, Ohio, to Kansas in the spring of 1902: land and prohibition. Though his family had been townspeople for several generations, he had a yearning for the land. As a staunch Presbyterian and a strict prohibitionist, he did not want his five sons and three daughters growing up in a state where alcoholic liquors were sold. Kansas had had a prohibition law since 1880, so at age fifty-five he sold his interests in the iron business, loaded his household goods on a freight train, and moved his family to Emporia, Kansas, a town chosen because it had a Presbyterian college. He rented a house, put his children in school, and looked for a farm.

A farm was found in Chase County with a five-hundred-acre pasture, four hundred acres of farming land, and a creek, the South Fork of the Cottonwood River. Even more important to him was the big rambling house. "I'll take it," he decided. "That house will hold all my children." (An orphaned nephew and niece were also sometimes members of his household.) The deed, signed on March 31, 1902, gave him "920 acres more or less" for sixteen thousand dollars.

E. B. Greene farmed by the book, subscribed to Hoard's Dairyman, and kept up a correspondence with the Kansas State Agricultural College in Manhattan, which issued bulletins on everything from wheat rust to chicken pip. In an area where grazing beef cattle was the main occupation, he decided to have a dairy herd of Holsteins. He installed milking machines and a Delco electric plant to provide power. The cream he shipped to a creamery station and the skim milk was fed to the hogs. In addition, his several hundred acres of land were farmed and the five-hundred-acre pasture rented out.

This was the Flint Hills of Kansas, a vast area of grazing land, of rolling hills covered with native bluestem grass which holds nutrients that will fatten cattle without additional grain. Flinty limestone just beneath the surface makes the land unsuitable for cultivation. Pasture once plowed does not return to native grass, nor is the land desirable for crops. Farming land lies along the streams.

We were to live with Willard's parents. His brother Churchill was in France in military service with the 35th

Infantry Division; another brother, Dwight, was working in Kansas City. Needing help with the farm, Willard's father had urged him to give up teaching. Temporarily, we thought. So Willard resigned his position as superintendent of schools in Florida and we became Kansas farmers.

The early settlers had planted the cottonwood around their houses because it was quick-growing. Its frilly daintiness must have warmed the heart of the pioneer woman and its soft rustle whispered to her of courage and faith.

I learned to love the cottonwood, the inspiration for our town's name. It is not a sturdy or long-lived tree, like the oak. Its wood is not valued, like the walnut's. It does not even make good firewood. But it has an airy grace that pays its way.

Through the heat of the summer it stands cool and clean and shining. Its leaves shake off dust as nervously as a fluttery housewife polishes the furniture, never content to sit for a moment with quiet hands. In the night it makes a rain-sound on the roof.

The cottonwood is a sympathetic tree, sensitive, brooding, like those yearning souls who love to bear burdens. It sighs as if in distress that man's progress through this vale of tears should be so vexing. But it never intrudes. It expresses its feeling in well-bred murmurs. It asks no questions, but tenderly flutters down its leaves. They fall as easily and copiously as a woman's tears, which, blotted and wiped away, start falling again with each new sigh.

A cottonwood is a tree to live with. I'm sure it is good luck to have it bless the hearth with a baptism of leaves for the first fire.

The four of us lived in the same house that summer and Churchill was an unseen fifth. With newspapers and maps, his father charted each location of the 35th and waited eagerly for letters from France. Then word came that he was hospitalized. In the battle of the Argonne Forest, shrapnel had hit his knee, news that brought concern and relief.

The house's large kitchen had a wood-burning range,

a sink with a cistern pump, a zinc-topped worktable, cupboards, and a big pantry. Off the kitchen the Greenes had a dining room with wide bay windows opening into the front hall, beyond which were double parlors, one with a fireplace. At the back of the house were a library and large bedroom occupied by Willard's parents. The bathroom had a zinc tub but no running water. A basement housed the furnace. Upstairs there were four bedrooms, and all over the house was solid walnut, marble-topped furniture.

The little town of Bazaar, a quarter of a mile from our place, was the end of the railroad. There were no "native" cattle. Those pastured in the area were shipped there, fattened during the summer, then sent to market by rail. In early years they had come on cattle drives. Now they arrived in trucks and stepped right out into grass which grew as much as eight feet tall in places.

Bazaar was a thriving small town with two grocery stores, a hardware store, post office, and a telephone exchange operated by the Henry McCracken family. You rang and asked for a name, not a number, and might be told, "She's not at home, Dear. I saw her go past a few minutes ago." Another time an unanswered ring might be explained, "I expect she's at her daughter's. The little girl's not well and they were taking her to the doctor this morning." Where, in the maze of area codes, dialing, and multiple digits can anyone get such service today?

I was the new girl in town and was soon meeting the neighbors. Will and Jessie Oles, an elderly couple with no children, ran a neat farm just across a field. They would invite us over to hear operatic records on their Victrola—Caruso, Farrar, Schumann-Heink, John McCormick—and sometimes we went with them on picnics.

I joined the Justamere Study Club in Cottonwood Falls, which met twice a month for papers and talks and play readings, with special topics for roll calls, one of which was "How was the weather on your wedding day?" When it came my turn to entertain, I turned once again to the agricultural college and received from the home economics department recipes for seafood casseroles. Something special was always served to complement the literary fare.

The neighbor women met at our house to sew outing flannel pajamas for the soldiers and I was asked to run the sewing machine, fitted with a little electric motor pushed under the wheel and powered by the Delco plant. We turned pajamas out by the dozens and I learned to make a neat welt seam. With several other women, I took a Red Cross course in nursing.

Willard got up early and with the help of a man employed on the farm would milk the cows, separate the cream, and feed the hogs before breakfast. It was always a hearty meal. There was oatmeal, put on the night before in a double boiler, followed by bacon or ham and eggs, with either pancakes or toast. Thick fresh cream was brought in and whole milk to drink. All of us drank milk.

But before breakfast there were always Bible reading and prayer. The family gathered in the dining room and Father Greene read from the Bible, sometimes dipping into the old Prophets, but the Sams—he gave the word Psalms a short a—were his favorite and the words rolled out in all the majesty of the King James version. With earnest faith he lifted his eyes unto the hills, sure that strength would be coming from the Lord who made heaven and earth.

The reading was followed by prayer, and the prayers were always the same. No pleas were made for good crops or needed rain or better markets. No personal favors were asked. The prayers were for the salvation of mankind. No matter if hay was down and rain threatened and the threshers were due, nothing interfered with or hastened morning worship, and any hired man or woman helper in the house was expected to kneel with the family.

Father Greene never sat down to eat—not even on the hottest day—without first putting on his coat, a thin gray alpaca which he kept hanging on the back of his chair. He served the food as he had done when his table was surrounded by children. His sons addressed him as Sir and gave him respectful attention. Nobody called him by his first name, nor did he address anybody by a first name except young people and his farm employees.

Though the Greene family was friendly with their neighbors, I soon learned their ways were different. In a farm community Sunday is a day for visiting, but for the Greenes it was a day for church and contemplation. Cooking was kept to a minimum and no farm work was done except the necessary attention to animals. Willard said that when he was a child they spent Sunday afternoons sitting in a circle, reading in turn from the Bible.

Father Greene lived by his beliefs in the Bible, the Presbyterian Church, and the system of supply and demand. He disagreed with local opinion that an abstract villain called Wall Street was responsible for the low prices of farm products. Always forward-looking and progressive, he was the first in the community to have silos and a telephone, stretching a wire on fence posts to bring the service to his house. At his own expense he dragged the dirt roads after a rain. He was an early owner of an automobile. When he was learning to drive, he drove into the old shed where the car was kept, found he could not stop, and went on through the back wall. Without fuss he circled around, entered again, and stopped promptly.

He accorded to his wife and all women the greatest consideration and courtesy, but expected them to stay put in their God-ordained places, which did not include the pulpit or the voting booth. No word of swearing, however mild, was heard in his house, no tobacco in any form was used, nor any reference made to any garment not visible or any part of the body thought to be indelicate. Mother Greene, if it became necessary to refer to the bull, called him "the gentleman cow."

While fitting ourselves into this pattern of living, Willard and I had a life of our own, almost as clandestine as though we were unmarried—quick kisses as we washed the cream separator, making a game of counting the disks, touching of hands, glances. What he could say with those great brown eyes, deep set in his face, had no need to be translated into meter or music.

On pleasant Sunday afternoons Willard and I sometimes walked alone in the woods along the creek that circled the cornfield, hand in hand, or we would sit on a rock and watch the water flowing. Once we had a secret adventure. Rains flooding the creek had set it rampaging. Trees normally on the banks were standing in water. Nevertheless, we got into a homemade boat for a romantic ride—and were swished uncontrollably down the creek. Only by catching hold of overhanging branches did we stay our progress and only by bracing the boat with the oars and pulling ourselves upstream branch by branch were we finally able to get back safely. Like guilty children, we did not have the nerve to tell of our escapade.

Our room was our world, where we lived evenings and Sundays. It had bird's-eye maple furniture, with much tatting on dresser scarves done by Mother Greene. Nothing in it was particularly our own, but its furnishings were of scant importance. We were there and it was ours.

It was a hot summer. Every animal sought the shade. Chickens dropped their wings and held their mouths open. Mother Greene sat calmly in the bay window tatting and saying periodically, "I think there's a little breeze coming in now." Willard would come in from the fields wet with sweat and gray with dust. I endured those days, wanting only for them to hurry on toward evening when the scorching sun would set. There was no shower, no cool summer clothing. Long skirts had been gone only three or four years; shorts and sandals were far in the future.

In this heat supper would often be noon leftovers supplemented with fresh fruit and vegetables. One evening Willard and I moved an old steel cot into the backyard and abandoned our hot bedroom. We washed the dishes and the cream separator and sat on the back porch as dusk settled down. Then in cool darkness we slipped into the cot under the trees and into each other's arms and, with the shrill cicadas dropping into a slower cadence, went to sleep. This was our real honeymoon, not those few awkward days at Wagonwheel Gap.

Chapter 25: Silver and Gold

*O*ne of my prized possessions is a battered old book in which I kept household accounts when we were first married. Fired with ambition to do my duty till it hurt, I laid a domestic map out under ten heads: "Groceries," "Clothing," "Postage," "Health and Beauty," "Recreation," "Equipment," "Domestic Service," "Insurance," "Dues," and a catch-all "Miscellaneous." Every cent we spent went into its proper column and had to be added both ways and balanced with "Cash on Hand" at the end of the month. For a few months it looked as though our marriage had deprived some deserving firm of a good bookkeeper.

But as time went on, my purchases tended to gravitate to two heads: "Groceries" and "Miscellaneous." Doubtless we still used postage, indulged in a little recreation from week to week, and squandered some of the egg money on "Health and Beauty," but the thing which we bought in a really big way was "Miscellaneous."

I would like you to believe that it was not in the spirit of vanity that I invented the column called "Health and Beauty." At first I called it just "Health," which was meant to include tooth paste, castor oil, and toilet soap. But in the meantime I was having difficulty placing face creams and powder under a proper head. I could not honestly make myself believe they were necessary to health. Ten heads seemed a suitable number, and, since the book was only so wide, I couldn't create another. I knew from the magazines that the only way to begin a happy married life was to be honest in all things, so I just added "Beauty" to "Health" and lumped castor oil and face cream in the same stall.

The record shows I kept account faithfully for five months, balanced like a circus acrobat; the sixth month was entered but not balanced; all entries stopped on the twenty-first of the seventh month. A few pages over I began keeping lists of manuscripts submitted to magazines—and returned. Several pages over I kept accounts with the newspapers I wrote for.

If this faithful account book survives my brief stay upon this whirling ball of futility and frustration, it will stand as a graphic biography of one who started things she couldn't finish. No other document will be necessary.

"Cash on Hand" I got from Willard's and Father Greene's books. A not insignificant amount came from our four large silos. A fall ritual was Father Greene's selling silage we did not need for our own stock to William Norton, the oldest member of a large pioneer family. On such occasions Mr. Norton was received with ceremony in the front parlor. At any other time he would have come to the kitchen door. (The front door of a farmhouse was for the preacher, peddlers, and visitors from town.) We could never hear what was said in the parlor, but we knew those two veterans were sparring, one intent on buying silage at as low a price as possible, the other intent on getting as much as he could. It always ended amiably in a figure acceptable to both.

Sale of livestock also brought in "Cash on Hand." Exciting were our trips to Kansas City in the caboose of the Santa Fe to sell a load of hogs. The market was watched days in advance and a time chosen. If prices were not satisfactory that day, we would wait for another in the hope that the market might improve enough to pay for another night in the pens. Selling was a guessing game and the man who hit a good market day had something to brag about.

Our boys came home from war, swinging off the train in khaki uniforms (complete with puttees) into welcoming arms. Churchill returned limping from his wound, throwing off his jacket which he declared would fit the radiator and saying he never wanted to taste salmon again in all his life.

On Thanksgiving Day 1919 the Greenes held a big family reunion: three daughters and three sons, whose new wives were looked over and sized up. Churchill and his wife Estelle came from Emporia, where he had re-entered college. There were two Marys. Mary and her husband, Donald Dougall, came from Maplewood, New Jersey. Dwight and his wife Mary came from Kansas City. And three Virginias showed up. Elizabeth Stewart and her daughter Virginia came from Tacoma, Washington. Willard's sister Virginia and her husband, L. F. Parrish, and their two children, also named Virginia and L.F., came from Metropolis, Illinois.

Put a few Greenes together and you have talk! Eddies and whirlpools of conversation formed and parted. Groups gathered, then merged and mingled like square dancers in a set. Long before the talk dwindled, parlors were turned into bedrooms and everybody had a place ready for sleep.

After the reunion, the Dougalls stayed all winter and we played games every evening—auction bridge, "500," and a Chinese game we ordered through the mail, Mah Jong, played with tiles involving an east wind, a west wind, and the dragon. In the midst of their happy, long visit a sad accident occurred. The Dougalls had brought with them a beautiful pedigreed wolfhound, which they left with us one weekend while they went to visit Churchill and Estelle in Emporia. The poor thing died after getting into poison Willard had put out for rats. I dreaded the Dougalls' return, but Willard, who never shrank from doing whatever had to be done, told them straight out. The news was received in shocked silence.

But that loss soon seemed minor. Willard's mother, who had not been well for some time, had returned to Illinois with her daughter to undergo diagnosis. It was found to be cancer. She remained with Virginia until her death a few months later on May 5, 1920. Father Greene accepted her going as he accepted whatever came, with no expression of grief except that which we could see written on his face.

No price can be set upon love. It is not a feeling that we bestow at will. We do not understand it, but we receive it with awe and wonder and rapture. It gives and gives but asks nothing in return. Yearning and inarticulate, it would gladly resolve itself into a golden stream to anoint the wounds of its beloved.

But when it is gone, it is gone and nothing can compensate for the loss of it. A man and a woman who have stood upon the mountain top of a love which gives and suffers and is patient, a love that must be fought for and struggled for, a love that sacrifices and protects, would know that it is the most precious thing in the world and cannot be gotten for gold, nor silver weighed for the price thereof.

Chapter 26: Growing Pains

*W*hen a woman learns she is pregnant for the first time, her feelings are mixed. Mingled with a quick surge of pleasure is the sense of embarking on a course that has no turning back. It is somewhat like having the restraining bar slammed shut on the seat of a roller-coaster or entering the first turbulence of rapids on a raft—you're in for it and there's nothing to do but hold on.

After several months Willard informed the doctor of our expectations. I did not go in for an examination. Instead, I sent off to the agricultural college for bulletins on prenatal and infant care, sent without cost, which I read carefully.

Since our child, like most, was to be born at home, arrangements were made with a nurse to stay a week after the baby's birth. In the meanwhile, I sewed long dresses of soft white cotton trimmed with "fencerow" embroidery. I made little slips called "gertrudes" which buttoned on the shoulders, and wrappers of outing flannel which buttoned down the front. As directed in the bulletins, I made dozens of dressings which had to be wrapped tightly in paper and sterilized in the oven. These wide bands were pinned about the abdomen of the newly born for a month or two. An infant coming from free-form floating in the womb apparently had to be made miserable by being popped into tight clothes as soon as possible after arrival.

My time arrived. Doctor and nurse were summoned in the evening. The doctor, saying it would be a while yet, went into another room to sleep. My pains came faster and worse—the roller-coaster was in one of its dips, the rapids tossing the raft. I clung thankfully to dear Frances Stubenhofer, the nurse.

On the morning of September 1, 1920, we had our first born, a daughter, beautiful from the very first look. We named her Margaret Louise. I showed her proudly to neighbors and every day gazed at her in wonder. My mother came to help care for her after the nurse left.

Margaret was a joy to all. Grandfather Greene wanted to feed her as soon as she was old enough to sit at the table in the little highchair made for him when he was a baby. As she grew older he took her nestled beside him in the Buick touring car on trips to town. By the end of her fist year she was talking a torrent, and before she was two she could call each Holstein by name. Independent, she insisted she could wash herself and wanted to put on her own clothes (once in a while she would get something on right). She peeled boiled eggs quite well, and before I thought it possible she was setting the table and handing me clothes to hang on the line. Willard began teaching her "mathematics," and she soon could identify one, two, or three objects, and sometimes four.

I wrote my parents on November 21, 1922: "This morning she said to me, 'Open your mouf so I can see your teef' and after a close examination said, 'I think it's about to come through. Have you a canine teef, Mama?' She is just getting her lower canines. Lest you think she is entirely angelic I will have to tell you that she showed an exhibition of temper the other day at the table that would do justice to all the greats on both sides." We were happy in our snug little Eden.

A few months before Margaret's second birthday, on May 20, 1922, we had another child. This time the doctor, having to traverse seven miles of muddy road, did not have to wait. The baby arrived before he did. Willard sat by in lieu of doctor and nurse. "We've got a son," he announced.

A daughter and now a son—our cup overflowed. We named

him Edward Barton Greene, maintaining the traditional E. B. Greene, but substituting "Edward" for "Elisha."

It was soon evident, however, that our baby was not well.

The doctor came several times before I was told the boy had been born with a defective heart. A valve between the two chambers which mixed the purified and unpurified blood had failed to close. The only hope Dr. Woodhull offered us was that he might grow out of it.

However faint a hope, people cling to it. We saw other doctors and specialists of course, but they had nothing more to give. "He might grow out of it."

Remedies were soon forthcoming from concerned people who knew nothing about medicine. One lady was sure the child's trouble could be cleared up with a daily dose of castor oil. Mrs. Oles, observing that he seemed to get better and worse regularly, offered the opinion that the moon caused his sickness.

Edward was a sweet child with soft golden hair and the big brown eyes that all the Greene children have, and we yearned with tenderness for him. Margaret was fond of carrying him from one member of the family to another. Although Dr. Woodhull seemed enthusiastic over the improvement in his heart, he remained quite conservative in his statements to us and we steeled ourselves for that time when we knew that he would leave us.

But we were ill-prepared for the shock of losing our little girl.

These many years afterwards I still feel the pain and grief of Margaret's death on December 15, 1922, three and a half months after she was only two years old. I still feel guilt at not having watched her more closely, my father's constant words of caution haunting me, accusing me. No doubt intending to help me, she pulled a scalding pot of water from the stove, too great a shock for her delicate system to sustain.

The old grandmothers were right: there are growing pains. Not just of the body, which are over in a few years, but those of the soul, which go on and on. Immunity is never established. With bitterness and pain each lesson is learned, is beat into our hearts with the hardness of experience. And each person must weather his own storms.

Sleepless nights of bitter anguish, tragic hours of walking the floor, back and forth, back and forth, bitter memories, terrifying thoughts, tremulous prayers, with a heart that is as a stone within the body, then at last—never quickly—a ray of hope, a promise of peace.

Those are the growing pains of the soul.

Her body was not taken from the house. I washed and dressed her for burial and laid her in a tiny casket on a table in the front parlor. Willard and I stood looking at her beautiful, still face. The tears of that day still burn my cheeks. . . .

We placed her doll beside her.

Willard and I, with Bess and Clarence McCracken, our friends who lived in the tenant house and who had loved Margaret, carried her to the country cemetery. There, in the family plot by the side of the road, we laid her to rest near her young uncle and grandmother. At home after the funeral, I found a little bell she had hung on the knob of a kitchen drawer, where it remained until the fire.

For many months I wished only that I could die.

I used to look ahead and realize miserably that I might live to be sixty years old. I was not yet thirty and the prospect of thirty more years filled me with terror.

I lost all interest in life, all hope, all ambition, weighted down in that dark grave of grief and despair. I went through each day with a dull, painless ache in my heart, marking time.

But I was young and it is impossible to crush youth for long. Although life and joy came back, I found many things had been left behind, and one of them was fear. When you have been where you no longer care to live, there is nothing to be afraid of anymore. The old fears of what people might do or think or say were gone. I became my own self. I was free.

Three years later our third child was born, Willard

Bennington Greene, a beautiful, sturdy baby with blue eyes and fair hair. Grandfather Greene loved to care for the boys while I was away for the afternoon. Some afternoons, for the sake of company, I went swimming. Women and children would meet at a certain place overhung by trees on the south fork of the creek where there was a clear pool. A few phone calls could round up a group of young mothers with the dispatch of assembling a militia in time of war. Babies in baskets and young children were left on a wide gravelly bank, attended by the swimmers in turn or by someone who couldn't swim that day.

About this time Willard tangled with our Holstein bull which turned suddenly, lifted him across his head, and smashed him against the crib. If the hired man had not been there with a pitchfork Willard might have been killed, but the worst injury was to the lower part of his face.

Our doctor drove him to Topeka for surgery. About a week later Willard arose one morning, left a note signed "Impatient," and came home. Like the rider thrown from a horse, he resumed handling the bull immediately, taking a lesson from the hired man, who carried a heavy stick to whack the animal over the head to discourage male arrogance.

All these years I had been thinking of writing, distressed that time was going by and I was not making a start. So I wrote short stories which I sent to the *Saturday Evening Post* and the *Ladies' Home Journal*, the top-paying publications of that time. The stories came back, of course, testifying to the good judgment of the editors.

Later I began writing a column, "Flint Hill Fantasies," for the weekly newspaper in Cottonwood Falls, the *Chase County Leader*. Reading the paragraphs of the columnists in the Kansas City papers, I was sure I could do as well if not better. So on the occasion of a county fair, I asked permission of the editor, W. C. Austin, to write about the fair for the small extra paper he distributed daily from the stands. Setting it late at night he gave me the name "Peggy," which I kept when, at his invitation, I continued to write each week.

Looking back over those first years' columns I find a good many poems, some rhymed, some free verse. A few are embarrassingly sentimental. Others have a lightly ironic twist at the end, but are no less embarrassing. On the other hand, some are not so bad.

My column caught on. Area newspapers asked to reprint it, paying me fifty cents a week, the most beautiful money I have ever earned. The column was frequently quoted, and I was invited to speak at the State Editorial Convention in Topeka. For the occasion I saved up butter and egg money and borrowed from the children's banks to buy a pancake hat which slouched toward my forehead. The first thing I noticed at the meeting was one identical to it. I didn't know whether to be proud to have a hat like that of an obviously affluent Kansas City editor's wife or to wonder if mine made me look as silly as hers did.

My talk, on the theme that a columnist gets her material from people when they aren't looking, was, I am told, the hit of the meeting, but it should be stated that the convention was rather dry, involving talks about circulation, advertising, linotypes, and difficulties in meeting the payroll. Editors were having a Depression too.

As a result of my talk, Ernest Tucker, a reporter from the *Kansas City Star*, came out to the farm to interview me. He arrived on a day when both children had whooping cough; two high school boys staying with us as hired help had the mumps. It soon became obvious to the young man that I had my hands full without writing columns and should be tending to family matters rather than granting an interview. Too, it was easy to see that, like others from the city who visited us, he felt the loneliness of the surrounding hills. He was polite enough not to question why we dwelt so far from civilization—unlike the woman from Topeka who, walking about the house wringing her hands, finally wailed, "How can you stand to *live* here?"

She did not understand that after living on prairies for a while they become a quality rather than a quantity. The prairies do not startle you with sudden vivid beauty as a turn in a mountain road can do. They do not dazzle you or exhaust you with excitement. There are no dramatic tricks.

The prairies are as patient as time and as mysterious as the stars, with as many moods as the wind, drawing you on, and suddenly you know that this is what you have wanted all your life. That knowledge comes as gently as the prairie dusk.

Chapter 27: The Fire

*F*ather Greene was accustomed to rising earlier than his usual hour during the winter months in order to start fires in the furnace and kitchen range. It was a kindness on his part to have the house toasty warm by the time we awakened. One December morning, exactly one week before Christmas, Willard ran in from the barn yelling that our house was on fire.

The fire, we later learned, had started in the attic from a defective flue and was consuming the parlor and upstairs bedrooms. I grabbed a water bucket and followed my husband to an upstairs already so full of smoke we could scarcely breathe. As Willard climbed through a window to examine the roof, I ran to phone for help, got our babies ready, and sent them with Mrs. Ed Bailey, who had just dropped by for milk.

Neighbors saw the smoke and were soon at the house, joined by others who had been alerted by the Bazaar telephone operator. Each new arrival, not seeing Edward and Willard, screamed above the roar of the fire, "Are the children safe?" Although flames were leaping and crackling and everyone knew the house was doomed, men drew water from the well and formed a bucket line.

A railroad crew going to work stopped their handcar and came to our aid. Those Mexican section hands were truly commendable. Afterwards we wondered how they managed to save the heavy kitchen range, which was full of fire at the time. But there it stood unscathed in the back yard.

I decided I would try to save a few things and carried out the babies' chest of clothes and a drawer from the china closet base containing our silverware. I don't know why I didn't save the other drawer, but I think I left to get some photographs from our room. I opened the dining room door, went into the hall, and was stunned to see smoke. It was almost as impenetrable to the eyes as a moonless, starless night. I couldn't breathe. My eyes smarted. I ran to the door, hoping to get a good breath of air, then ran into our room. After two or three attempts to get inside, I gave up, went outside to the north window, and tried to pry the screen off, but found it too securely fastened. Running around the house to the east, I found men looking at the porch, some running around asking, "Where is Willard?" I was frozen with fear until he appeared from somewhere.

I have a vague memory of taking out things in a kind of trance but recall distinctly the ceiling burning overhead, dropping down to ignite the floor. I remembered Willard once saying in case of fire he would rather save his records than anything else, so I tried to rescue them. They were in my desk. The Little Leather Library on top and one edge of the desk were blazing. Pushing the little books to the floor, why I don't know, I pulled the desk away from the wall, but it caught on the linoleum and fell over, scattering into the flames Grandmother Greene's little candlestick, Kodak negatives of the babies' pictures, and most of the records I had meant to save. I remember sitting on the floor with everything lying within easy reach but being unable to get to them, as if I had lost all power of motion. When the little desk was carried out, its remaining drawer, too tight to fall out, held only the records of our registered Holsteins. For days the sight of that desk was a misery and reproach to me.

Few things were saved from that house my husband's people had lived in for a quarter of a century: a little walnut marble-topped chest, an upholstered chair, a platform rocker, the zinc-topped kitchen table, and drawers from a heavy sideboard. Everything else was lost—dishes, bedding, furniture, the winter coat my mother had just given me for Christmas. I stood and watched the head of my new sewing machine fall into the flames. All the clothes we had left were those we had on, or so we thought. Later returned to us was a basketful which had been sent out to be laundered.

When it was long over we wondered what had been in the boxes of unopened Christmas presents. At the time, we were unable to grasp the enormity of the loss, and our first thoughts were for little things. Father Greene said to me as we stood watching the ruins, "I hadn't finished the trip through Africa, was just at the Victoria Falls." He referred to an article in the *National Geographic* which he had not completed reading.

I hurried over to the Oles with Father Greene to see how Mrs. Bailey was making out with my babies. Young Willard's bottles had been lost in the fire and in the excitement no one thought to go get new ones, but he sat stoically and did not cry. Father Greene left for town at once. Later I realized that that poor little baby had gone nine hours without food. Toward the last, he sucked his thumb and looked solemn, while I kept my eye on the road. Finally new bottles came, were sterilized, and Willard was fed. Edward was equally calm, eating food offered him and making no fuss.

Kind and wonderful neighbors arrived, bringing dishes, bedding, towels, food, and by night we were moved into our tenant house, vacant that season. Father Greene and the children—somebody brought cribs for them—slept in the main room with its tiny stove. Willard and I slept in an icy bedroom under mountains of covers, warming each other. For a long time afterwards I would wake in the night, tense at any sound.

I went to midnight mass with the McCabes on Christmas Eve, but was so worn out that I was lulled to sleep by Father Disselcamp's Latin. I thought his services would never end. On Christmas morning Father Greene stayed in bed with a pain in his chest and a bad cough. I called Dr. Woodhull and was glad to learn there were no signs of pneumonia, though the doctor felt it could easily turn into that. We kept analgesic balm and a hot stove lid on his chest (our hot water bottle had burned). Before Monday came, Father Greene said he was well.

My wedding dress burned in the fire—along with Mrs. Will McCabe's, which needs explaining. My friend Maggie had borrowed the McCabe wedding dress for someone to wear in an old-fashioned pageant given by the women of the Farmers' Union. No one was slim enough to wear it except me—and the waist was tighter than I cared to admit. It was an amazing corded poplin-blue with a large bustle, red ruffle, an inside girdle of stays, large puffed sleeves, and an enormous white satin front (which I had to pad). With it I wore one of those hats that looks like an elaborately frosted chocolate cake. Will came up afterwards and said I looked nicer than anyone else. He seemed puzzled, though, when I asked if I might take the gown home to have my picture taken in it. It turned out he didn't know the dress was his wife's or that Maggie had "borrowed" it while he was away from home. I thought the situation a bit delicate, what with his poor wife being in an asylum, but Maggie assured me he would never know. Perhaps that was true, but I still feel like an accomplice in a crime every time I think of it.

We bought a few pieces of furniture, including a sewing machine—a fine old treadle that had sewn enough seams to reach around the earth at its middle with enough to spare to tie a bow. In the spring we hired Will Oles, a carpenter as well as a farmer, to build us a quick house of two rooms near our old site since the tenant house would be needed for a hired man or two. The old garage, which escaped destruction, he finished up as a bedroom for Father Greene, who steadfastly refused the urgent invitations of his daughters to go to one of their homes.

We found we could live in two rooms about as well as in eleven, with indeed some advantages—fewer rooms to clean, no unnecessary furniture, clothing, dishes, or ornaments to care for. Many things were gone which no one wanted but which we would have hesitated to destroy, mellow old things that had been full of tender memories for someone now long gone. The accumulated clutter of two or three generations was disposed of in a roaring conflagration which lasted only a few hours. We would not have known what to do with it. It would have filled up useful space for years. Now it was gone and no feelings hurt. We had nothing that we did not need and use.

Chapter 28: A Death and a Birth

*I*n the beginning, except for the newspapers, we hardly knew there was a Depression. We lived as we always had, nourished with our own milk, chickens, and garden. We had a house and clothes on our backs, and certainly were not out of work. But soon there were signs.

Nobody in our community was jumping out of high windows, but men began coming to the back door asking for something to eat, saying they were on their way to the harvest fields or some indefinite job, meaning that in the past they had not gone around asking for food. We always had something for them, and I tried to make neighborly talk to cover our mutual discomfort.

The citizens of Chase County went to their Bibles and many seemed to have opened it at First Corinthians 9:24: "So run that ye may obtain." Election year brought out candidates in droves. The modest pay of a county office for the first time in years was enticing. My husband was among the dozen or so who ran for county clerk. Candidates made daily rounds of the farm houses and knocked at front doors. A candidate seemed to hate to admit it was a nice day, for fear someone would point out that an opponent disagreed with him.

One candidate told us that while he was driving along in his Ford a giant of a fellow came tearing down the road in an enormous sedan and not only crowded him into a ditch but smashed a fender and locked bumpers. The candidate, remembering only that the highway hog was also a voter, smiled cheerfully and got out to apologize. "Then I saw he was carrying a Butler County license tag," he said, "and I sure gave him hell!"

A Democrat was elected. Willard, like most candidates in Chase County, was a Republican. He did not, like one defeated candidate, confide that he had been getting "awful tired" of shaving and dressing up every day.

When the price of butterfat dropped lower and lower and the livestock market went nowhere but down, we knew something was happening out there. Perhaps Wall Street was the culprit after all as the papers reported. Economies of our own could always be managed, but a mortgage company could be appeased only by cash.

Most farmers hated mortgages worse than original sin, but Father Greene, vice-president of the bank in Cottonwood Falls, viewed debt as a normal incident of business. In the land boom after World War I he had sold his five-hundred-acre pasture for as much as he had paid for the entire farm. As in prosperous years, he wore his clothes year after year and bought nothing for himself. He was generous in meeting what he considered his obligations—sending money to his children when they needed help, giving to church and missions, and providing for elderly spinster relatives.

If Father Greene had an extravagance it was his farm. He was always looking for better machines and more efficient methods. Some years before when farmers were signing leases for oil drilling, he said, "I'd rather they found a good well of water." (The well in the pasture, operated by a windmill, went dry in prolonged droughts and cattle had to be driven twice a day to the creek for water.) But nevertheless, "I'd rather live the way we are," he said, "than in the finest mansion in town." Now here he was with a mortgage nipping at his heels and the placating money nowhere in sight. Father Greene's distress touched me deeply and I wished earnestly that I had money to give him.

I saved box tops and entered contests, writing in twenty words why I liked a product, but won no prizes. I did win some at the county fair—for canning, pickling, preserving, and sewing, even once for butter—often ten to a dozen prizes which could add up to maybe fifteen dollars, a nice piece of money. I would hurry to the fair the day after judging to see which, if any, of my jars or sewing bore the coveted ribbon.

The mortgage caused us halfway jokingly to hope for heavy rain. The Greenes had kept the local weather station for years, recording the general face of the day, low and high temperatures, and precipitation. Any time an inch of more of rain fell in twenty-four hours we reported it and were paid a dollar.

Somehow we managed. Willard borrowed to the limit on his life insurance and sold the property he owned in Florida. One year a small loan was secured from the widow of Father Greene's brother, a canny, no-nonsense woman who came out of New Jersey to look at the farm. I had never met Aunt Hattie, but Willard had lived in her home, milked her cows, and done chores for her when he was a prep student at Princeton. His memories were of a woman whose table marked her as extremely frugal and thrifty.

Father Greene met her at the railway station and, to acquaint her with the general prosperity, took her to see the stores in Cottonwood Falls, of which he was volubly proud. "We've got some fine stores, Hattie," he said, leading her into Jim Bell's men's clothing store. "I didn't come all the way out here to see country stores, Barton," she said. "Now take me to your place." She was probably the only person in the world who called him Barton.

When another child was on the way, we bought a vacated country schoolhouse, moved and attached it to our two rooms. It made a big bedroom for ourselves and one for Father Greene. There was ample room for everyone.

I had by now learned to distrust happiness. It is the up end of the teeter-totter, and I knew as sure as fate that when the view was high and handsome we were due for a swift descent.

Nevertheless, too soon what I had always dreaded happened. No matter how much we thought we were prepared for it, we weren't.

Edward died when he was seven years old, on September 7, 1929. A bright and beautiful child, he had had no chance at life. It is still a sadness. I had no heart to write of his death in my column; I really have no heart to write of it now.

Three months later Dorothy Anne was born, beautiful, too, with great brown eyes. Young Willard had measles and was not allowed in the room with the baby. He would stand yearningly at the door in his sleepers, his sweet face splotched with red, until Father Greene came to trundle him off to bed.

Several weeks later I was up and about. One morning, after getting vegetables from the garden for dinner, I came into the kitchen and laid them on the table. I hurried to start a fire in the range. But that fire was never started, for, as I reached for an old newspaper, I saw a snake crawling along the woodbox. I was frozen stiff with horror. But I was not rooted to the floor—far from it.

Letting out a wild yip, I ran into the bedroom and jerked my sleeping baby from her crib, grabbed her brother by the hand, and fled. Outside, I loaded the children into the Model T touring car, which for a wonder started at once, and drove frantically in search of my husband. The baby was warm and drowsy from her nap, her hair clinging in damp curls, and her brother, sensing my fright, sat solemn and big-eyed beside me.

My husband calmly tied up the horses and came to the house with me. I stood outside clutching the children, petrified like the statue of the pioneer mother, while he, armed with a stick, went inside to search for the snake.

"Are you sure you saw one?" he wanted to know when he failed to locate it. Then indeed did terror seize me. I would never enter that house again, I declared, until that snake was found, removed, and destroyed. Quickly I ran over the names of our neighbors—the Oles, the Norths, the McCabes, the Baileys, the Gaddies—checking them off on my fingers. I felt sure any of them would take us in for an indefinite stay in such an emergency.

My thoughts were interrupted by a determined whacking inside the house. In a minute my brave husband emerged with a fourteen-inch monster hanging limply over his stick. I have never shaken my fear of snakes.

Soon young Willard was to have a birthday. A pup had been promised him for the important occasion. We read, researched, and compared breeds so that he might get the Perfect Boy's Dog. One day we favored a Scotch terrier, the next an Airedale, then wavered between a buff or a white Collie, while all the time I knew a Saint Bernard would add distinction to our establishment. One morning, weeks before the birthday, there appeared at the door, wagging his tail in a jolly manner, a humble dog of suspicious parentage. I said he must go; young Willard obviously felt it was an answer to his prayer; my husband said he looked like a nice dog and probably combined the best of all breeds. I insisted that he must not be fed or encouraged, but our son already had a piece of bread in hand and I weakened when I saw the look in the boy's and dog's eyes. I knew we now had a dog, a Perfect Boy's Dog.

Chapter 29: The Farm Woman

Father Greene, who had diabetes, died on his farm on July 23, 1930, a man loved and respected. All through his eighty-one years, in good times and bad, he had lived by his own standards, and nothing ever changed them. In the year following his death Willard sold the farm, or rather traded it for another one of lesser value, the trade providing money to pay our debts. We moved to a farm several miles away on a small stream called Buck Creek.

An advantage of owning few possessions comes at moving time. We had no fine china, crystal, linens, or paintings to pack. An old Kodak picture shows our meager household goods loaded on a single wagon with the family standing by, squinting into the sun. Somehow, from this long view backwards, the picture does not reflect our memory of ourselves. A stranger seeing it might take us for a saddened family being dispossessed. That is far from the truth. We entered our new life with zest and determination, with anticipated pleasure of a new home. The house, square and two-storied, had as much room as the one that had burned—larger rooms and higher ceilings. The living room was bordered at the top of the walls with elegant, wide, carved plaster, tinted blue. Both the dining room and the bedroom above it had large bay windows. There was a big bathroom with a zinc tub supplied with cold water from a cistern pump. Our few things were dwarfed in this spaciousness but we loved the big rooms. We even gave the children a playroom of their own. There, we reasoned, they could keep their toys, which, as a bonus, would never have to be picked up. It didn't work out that way, though. Children like to be where the action is. They and their toys were seldom in their playroom.

The Depression brought a jewel of a hired hand to our new home, a young man who had once made high wages as an oil driller. But now no one was drilling for oil. We had little money to pay, but, since he needed a place and we needed help, he worked for modest wages and lived as a member of our family, making enough to keep himself in tobacco and to celebrate a little on Saturday nights. Fancying a poker game and a bottle of whiskey, he was neither evasive nor apologetic about either. Nor were his high spirits, his poise, and his self-respect dampened on the one occasion when he was confined for a night in the local jail. He came home Monday morning as jauntily as ever.

He was excellent at any kind of work. He even liked to cook. His specialty was soup, but before he would start he had to shoo me out of the kitchen, certainly not a difficult matter. When he had finished stirring and seasoning, the result was fit for a king, though perhaps the soup was flavored additionally by my gratitude.

With his help we papered two big rooms. No matter what he did, he was witty and charming. We loved having him, as did several young ladies in the community. One day, though, he announced he would be leaving at the end of the week. He didn't have any particular place he was going or plans for that matter, he said, but it was time to move on. I washed and mended his clothes, paying particular attention to a lavender shirt that was his pride.

He did not go alone. The roads were filled with people heading west. One day we saw a man and a woman and four small children with a rickety two-wheeled cart in which the man was pulling the children. Going downhill, the woman sometimes rode and rested her feet, but uphill she walked and carried the baby, for the man was so weak that he could barely struggle between the shafts of the cart. A crude shelter of gunnysacks furnished their only protection from the scorching sun. It was obvious that they had known discouragement, poverty, hunger, disillusionment, despair, but now they could no longer afford emotions. There was only dull and tragic indifference on their faces.

It may be that all men are created equal and endowed with the rights of life, liberty, and the pursuit of happiness. Well-fed, secure persons may pursue happiness, but the sad-faced caravans which tramped the roads and highways were struggling for life itself, for food to maintain bare existence. The right to pursue happiness was too great a luxury for them. Had someone failed to be his brother's keeper? Had our country's rulers tossed these helpless wrecks into their last refuge, the open highway?

We felt fortunate to be secure, though poor. Our joys were simple. A hedge of ancient lilacs bordered one side of the yard and April brought the nearly unbearable beauty of this loveliest of spring flowers. After supper we sat with the children on the back porch, stunned by the fragrance that seemed to be a part of the soft dusk. Our house was surrounded by green pastures rolling off to a far blue haze on the horizon and, though there were neighbors, not a house could be seen. A stone fence, built in the days when men had more time than money, outlined the road and enclosed the barn. Walks about the place disclosed surprises of grassy creek banks and patches of wild flowers.

One evening as I was washing dishes young Willard came in and said, "Shut your eyes and don't look." He led me outside. At his command, I opened them to a hillside covered with lines of fire: a neighbor was burning his pasture in early spring. Flames crackled as the lines turned, receded, advanced, died out, and flamed up again. The boy held my hand, looking in wonder. The next morning the pasture was clean and black, waiting for grass to cover its hillsides as it had these thousands of years.

There may be little of conscious poetry in the feeling of a farm woman for nature, but I know there is great respect. They are partners, the woman and the elements, in the earnest business of making a living. She may relax and enjoy nature in its playful moods, but she knows that any minute she may have to draw and defend herself. Like a pet lion cub, it is nice when nature is frisky, but it bears sharp watching.

The city woman takes a little run out into the country with the expressed purpose of admiring the landscape, but to the lady on the land who lives with it every day the scenery is part of her very existence. Take rain. No other manifestation of nature causes so much emotion on the farm as rain or its lack. To others it may be only a matter of immediate discomfort, but a farm woman can witness a rain with a passion worthy of the grand operatic roll of Jovian thunderbolts.

She wastes no time in poetic outbursts, however. When a cold wind surges through the house and a blackish yellow cloud bears down from the northwest she doesn't stop to thrill before the angry saffron turmoil. There is too much to do.

It may be that after the windows have been closed, little chickens safely sheltered (no job for either a saint or a poet), the downspout flushed out and water pouring sweetly into the cistern, she may pause for a fantasy about the oblique silver curtain of rain, but it is much more likely that she will be on her way to the south bedroom with a dishpan to place under a leaky spot in the roof. By that time the family will be running to demand dry socks, shirts, and underwear, which may call for a little hasty needlework. Her thoughts, as she hurries about these chores, are only indirectly related to poetry. She may fear that a hard, driving rain has beaten off the strawberry blooms or killed the young lettuce, but over and above all she is thankful that the corn can resume its growth, that the new heads of wheat can fill out.

The farm woman has respect for cold and snow. At the first ominous signs of a winter storm she snaps into her routine like a professional dancer. Turkeys and chickens are driven to shelter, coal and wood carried in, and, if a severe freeze is threatened, vegetables are parked around the kitchen range and behind the wood heater.

She is not without appreciation of the beauty of the soft swirl of white about her or the stinging sharpness of sleet. She regards the storm as a respected foe, judging it, measuring it, calculating its fury, not looking at it through glass from a warm room.

But it is spring with its tender green shoots, its first pale spears of winter onions, that fills a farm family with a joy both passionate and lyrical. The warmth of spring sunshine means little chickens will not squawk and shiver, that gardens can grow, clothes will dry. Sometimes I think the most poetic heights reached by a farm woman are on washday. She has been known to write poetry about that. The sunniest and bluest of skies, the gentlest and softest of breezes, a taut clothesline on a hill high above the world, plus a cistern full of fresh rainwater—and washday, even with a hand-run machine, is something a queen may envy.

Then there are those fine sunshiny mornings with birds singing and fragrance oozing from the honey locusts when every excuse is seized to stay out of doors. It is so much more pleasant than washing the cream separator. It is easy at such times to remember so many things that need looking after— the asparagus may be large enough to eat, the rhubarb must need tending, new hens' nests should be made, and it seems vitally necessary to know if the corn is up and how much the wheat has grown since yesterday.

Outside work on the farm is not the hardship imagined by those who have not tried it. Hoeing in the garden among nesting birds is a pleasure on which housework must wait. And on a soft, dusky evening when the air is laden with lilac and humming with mystery, milking becomes a rite with the smell of fresh milk and the comfortable warmth of the cow's side as overtones to the tune of milk hitting the pail.

The cheery song of the cardinal always brings a farm woman to the window to search for the flaming spot he makes on a dull tree. And I have known a woman to walk half a mile every morning to meet the mail carrier so he would not have to disturb four small blue-green eggs incubating inside the mail box with a deplorable lack of respect for strict postal laws.

The farm woman is too close to nature to regard it as a separate phenomenon. She sees it, hears it, smells it, feels it, becomes part of it. Sunshine and rain, cold and wind and storm, birds and all growing things are not just something to talk about or write about, but something to live with, to use, to enjoy, to conquer, to endure, to love.

Chapter 30: A New Season

One can never know what a day will bring. People may lay their lives out in patterns of their own choosing, but those patterns cannot always be followed. I was in the midst of the washing one Saturday morning, when I received a phone message that our son had been thrown from a horse. His arm was broken.

Hurrying to drive him to a hospital in Emporia, I left the house in a state of suspended animation with half-laundered clothes soaking in the washing machine and a half-cooked dinner cooling on the back of the stove. I forgot entirely the carload of Missouri relatives at that moment motoring across the state toward our farm.

My guests, finding no one home, sat down to wait. Hours later my husband returned. He found my hastily scribbled note and put them up for the night. They left the next morning, saying they would stop again on their way back from Colorado.

It had been lonely and sad, leaving little Willard at the hospital. Coming home I found an empty house in which so short a time ago he noisily rode through the rooms on his tricycle, his sister behind him on an improvised rumble seat. Could I possibly have ever reprimanded him to "ride someplace else"? He teased me on Saturdays to "stop writing the Peggies and read Uncle Wiggily" until I was glad when he went out to play and left me in peace. My guilt was lessened only by the thought that on the morrow I would be off to Emporia again to keep him company.

He was not the forlorn waif I expected to find. He was, in fact, quite content. His pain forgotten, he had fallen in love with his nurse, who—he insisted—looked just like the lady on the Sears, Roebuck catalogue. I could not recall offhand just who graced that cover. "Oh, you know," he said, "the lady on Bedloe Island holding up the torch."

Impressed with the wide expanse of grass surrounding the hospital, he thought they ought to keep cows on it. So did we, and the hospital graciously accepted a calf as part payment for his treatment.

A week later my Missouri relatives returned as promised, refreshed and expecting a visit, but I had taken young Willard—we now called him "Brother" to avoid confusion—to the hospital to have his arm reset. Again my relatives sat down and waited. Eventually my husband came back and put them up for the night. They left the next morning without having seen me. Both times they cooked meals for themselves and my abandoned husband. This, I felt, was an ideal way to entertain. A cynic has said that relatives visit to inspect your housekeeping. They can do this much more satisfactorily in your absence.

The election of 1932 elicited great excitement throughout the state, especially the gubernatorial race. Dr. John R. Brinkley, noted for his goat gland rejuvenation operations, was running against the incumbent Harry Woodring, Ben Paulen, and the state's favorite son, Alf Landon. In August Dr. Brinkley appeared on the lawn of the Chase County courthouse. Business was rejuvenated right away. Merchants became exhausted from waiting on crowds of customers.

"Doc" sailed up majestically in a sixteen-cylinder Cadillac. He boasted that he had four more cylinders than the Governor and intended to keep a few cylinders ahead of all the other candidates. I had been impressed with Landon and wrote, "If it wasn't for the expense of that new baby, Nancy Josephine, Alf Landon might be able to afford a steam calliope to tour the state also, but, alas, babies cost money, and the upkeep of an oil well keeps one awake nights; so Alf may have to keep those battered old cars the *Kansas City Star* interviewer saw cluttering up his place in Independence."

Brinkley, immaculate and elegant in a white suit, was not the emotional thespian I had envisioned. There was little dramatic appeal in his address, which he delivered seated at a microphone. His attention centered on his hands. The crowd seemed more curious than enthusiastic. Although there was no unusual demonstration during his talk, it was startling to see the crowd almost mob him as he left the platform. People with faces shining in the hot sun fought to shake hands with the "next governor." It made one think of the mob pressing around to touch the hem of His garment.

The quality most lacking in Brinkley was the one most evident in Alf Landon—sincerity. Landon's was the clear, direct speech of an earnest man talking to friends. He made no extravagant promises. He said simply that government must adopt the methods and economies that private businesses had been forced to adopt. He stressed that a governor was not an inspired monarch, but one of the people who needed help and advice to carry on the complicated business of the state. Alf Landon prevailed in the avalanche of sweeping Democratic victories and gave Republicans at least one reason to celebrate.

My editor, Mr. Austin, successfully ran for the office of state printer. He offered Willard, with whom he served on the school board, a job in his Topeka office. So Willard went to the state capital, returning almost every weekend, and I stayed on the farm with the children and the two high school boys who helped with the work. Since our farm was to be rented to a neighbor at the end of the summer, we had a sale to dispose of our stock and farm equipment. The day was radiant.

There is always a definite date, a certain day, when summer turns into fall—and it does not depend on the calendar. But sometime, usually during the last week of August, the hot stillness of summer is broken by a thin, moaning breeze which gives one the eerie feeling that it is from another world. It sighs through the trees and presently there are a few leaves on the ground.

After that, the sunlight is mellow gold, flooding the earth with soft light. One seeks its warmth instead of the shade. The nights are cool. Blankets and coats come out. The sun lolls in bed later and later, for it too seems to feel that winter is coming.

This pale, glowing amber is a period of armistice, a truce between summer and winter, a warning that snow will cover the earth, that sharp winds will whistle through the bare trees, a warning to prepare. These are golden days to put away food, to gather fuel, to arm oneself against the long, bitter cold.

Summer is waving a far-off goodbye, pleading for the earth to wait, to be patient, to understand, to remember that she will come again. In the other distance, Winter is champing restlessly at the delay, eager to pounce upon the world, to fling his winds against it, to pelt it with whirling snow, and to roar through the trees in a laughing blizzard, hurling the last defiant leaves to the ground. But now there is peace and calm and quiet between these two ancient enemies. It is the golden truce.

That day had arrived.

After the sale we stood sadly in our house of tall, silent rooms. We saw so many things we had meant to mend, a torn strip of wallpaper, the little corner chipped out of a window pane. Here, the smudge of small hands on the walls where the animal alphabet had hung; there, the recorded heights of our children.

We moved hurriedly through memory-haunted rooms. It is best not to stay long in a house one has vacated. We closed the door and went away.

Part IV.

Topeka, Kansas, 1933-1943

Chapter 31: The Drought

*H*ot and cold running water—that is what marked the difference for me between country and city living. In our neat little two-story, five-room house at 1334 Euclid Avenue we had running water at the kitchen sink and in the bathroom. I felt a kind of guilt at having water flow in and out of our house with the turn of a faucet when I knew friends at home were still drawing water from a cistern, lugging it to the house, and carrying it out again when used—rain or shine, heat or cold, sick or hale.

Nothing eases day-to-day living quite so much as hot and cold running water. It eliminated the need for a little facility out back. (Jokes about privies were numerous, but never funny to people who used them.)

Brother insisted on two baths a day—at first—but soon the novelty wore off. No sooner would I get into the tub, however, than the telephone would ring. On the farm one could arrange a bath in comparative privacy with dignity. You called up the girl on the switchboard and said, "Mary, I'm going to take a bath. If anyone calls, find out who it is." Or, you phoned a woman on your party line and said, "The bath water's warm, Ella, and if our phone rings, please answer it and see what's wanted." But there was no way on earth to prevent the ringing of a dial telephone.

Stimulated by the conveniences of city living, I flew

at the housework, cooking, washing dishes, making up beds, sweeping and dusting, washing and ironing, sewing, shopping. Without chickens or garden, with no wood or coal to carry in or ashes to carry out, with no lamps to clean and fill, tending house seemed more play than work. It is hard to describe the delight and astonishment that filled those days. Press a button and there was light! We soon had an electric iron and toaster. For a few months I must have come near to qualifying as the perfect housewife. Never before had I kept house so well, and never have I since.

Some things did not change greatly. We brought from the farm our hand-turned washing machine and oak ice box. But now ice was delivered to us, the amount indicated by a card placed in the front room window. An ice man, protected by a leather apron, lifted out a large, silvery block with his tongs, slung it over his shoulder, and carried it into the house. I would run to open the box, hastily wipe away any spilled milk, and comment that the ice must be heavy. Since we did not lock our doors, if I was not at home he let himself in and put the ice in the box. I don't remember how much he was paid, but I am sure that it was not as much as he deserved.

I generally followed Alexander Pope's admonition not to be the first to try the new nor the last to desert the old, but it was with great reluctance that I gave up the ice man and our ice box, sorry to lose the shining block of ice against which jello would solidify while meat was cooking and milk would stay icy cold. We bought an electric refrigerator, secondhand, topped by a fixture that reminded me of Saturn's rings.

Willard went off to work mornings in a suit instead of overalls, carrying a sack lunch. When he came home at night, his working day was over. With no hogs to feed, no milking to do, no chickens to pen up, he spent his late afternoons reading, writing letters, doing accounts, listening to the radio, or walking about the neighborhood. It was the first time in our married life that we had leisure. It was like another honeymoon.

My column in the weekly *Chase County Leader* had become

fairly well known in the five years I had been writing. When the editors using my weekly column learned I was moving to Topeka, they offered advice and comment: "I'm afraid if you go there, you will lose your country touch" or "Keep writing like you do and don't go mingling with politicians." A few months after our move to town I was given a chance, "on trial," to write a daily column for the *Topeka Capital*. The *Capital*'s editor invited me to attend the Finney bond scandal trial and write, not the news, but my impressions.

Ronald Finney had been a prominent banker, a pillar in the community, a solid citizen, a church and civic leader. He conspired with the State Treasurer—elected by the people to serve the people—to remove government bonds and other negotiable paper from the State's vault and peddle it back East. The vault was seldom looked into by anybody and had been well looted before the loss was discovered. The trial, at which both men were convicted and sentenced to the penitentiary, rocked the state.

While attending the trial, I needed somebody in the house—Dorothy Anne was not yet in school. I advertised in the papers and interviewed several who wanted jobs, including a professional maid. She let it be known at the start that, until now, she had worked for only the "best people"—but they being somewhat down on their luck, she might consent to work temporarily in a lower stratum. Of course, she was not used to doing laundry. The best families sent theirs out and, furthermore, she could never risk her health by hanging out clothes in winter.

She informed me she had not previously considered working for what we were able to pay, but... She gave the impression she would be doing us a big favor in consenting to take our offer. But first she wanted to know if she would have a bath. Yes, indeed, I said graciously, she could have a bath whenever she felt she needed one. We didn't always wait until Saturday night ourselves. But it seems that she expected a private bathroom. (To me, a woman who had spent practically all of her life carrying water into the house and bathing in a washtub behind the kitchen stove, our one shared bathtub was still a luxury.) It would have been nice to have learned more about how the best people lived, but I knew we would be a big disappointment to the girl, so I didn't engage her services.

Fortunately we received a letter from a woman back home whose husband had been connected with a bank that failed, asking if she might stay with us for a while and help with the work. We settled on three dollars a week—which delighted her since she had not expected pay. But that meant another bedroom, which we did not have. While walking around the neighborhood one evening, Willard met a nice elderly gentleman, W.A. Neiswanger, who lived at 1601 Mulvane, a large house he had built a block from the Washburn College campus. Since only his room and a small upstairs apartment were occupied, he offered us the downstairs and three bedrooms upstairs for twenty-five dollars a month. We moved in gratefully and lived there until we bought a house of our own at 1205 Mulvane six years later for five thousand dollars.

I continued with my weekly columns for the country papers and, after the bond scandal trial, was hired to write a column for the *Capital* six days a week. I soon learned that writing a column was a quick way to learn about a town and its people.

It was with some hesitation that I accepted an assignment to visit a transient camp run by the government for homeless and jobless men. Here I was, a woman who had a job, coming to ask questions of men who didn't. Who could blame them if they resented it? But what I found were people temporarily stranded, waiting for the wreck to be cleared away, and accepting the situation with good humor. A lawyer and an accountant were washing dishes, a former stockbroker was putting food away, and a Notre Dame graduate was looking after a man who was sick. They were joking and laughing. A radio was playing. Men read books and magazines, worked puzzles. A man tore a cigarette paper, put half of it back in the book and rolled a cigarette with the other half. Then I realized the truth of that old adage about trouble shared. Seeing others in the same misfortune as himself, a man can salve his hurt in knowing "if it also happened to all these others, maybe it isn't all my fault that I am here." To pay for their care, the men each worked twenty-four hours a week and could work additional time for spending money.

The market for used clothing was brisk. Needing a winter coat, I looked through the paper and found an ad that seemed promising. I drove to the address, a comfortable two-story house, and recognized the woman who answered my ring. I instantly wished myself elsewhere. I had met her only a few days earlier at a political tea and we had conversed brightly with each other on a high plane, she the wife of a judge, I the new columnist becoming known about town. Now here she was, selling last year's coat, and I, coming to buy it—each of us embarrassed by this unexpected encounter. She began offering reasons for selling the coat, reasons why I could hardly find it suitable. I began trying to think of favorable things to say about it while explaining why it was not exactly what I needed—a strange dialogue between a seller and a prospective buyer. Of course we both should have acknowledged the situation and had a good laugh, but neither of us was quite up to that. Finally I managed to get out of the house after strained attempts at polite conversation on an elevated plane.

Although the Depression may have been caused by the stock market crash in New York, in Kansas the 1930s are remembered for their excessive heat and severe drought which caused dust storms that devastated the western part of the state. Temperatures moved past a hundred, not just for a day or two, but for weeks at a time. The summer of 1936 had nine days registering over one hundred and ten degrees, thirty over a hundred and five, and fifty-four over a hundred. That summer set forty-one new heat records. The hottest day was one hundred and fourteen degrees, July 24. There was no air-conditioning; electric fans whirred feebly day and night. It was the summer our Kansas governor, Alfred M. Landon, was nominated for president on the Republican ticket and the national press came for the notification. At a luncheon for a visiting presswoman, a big block of ice was set in a tub in front of a fan to blow coolness into the room. At the newsroom on hot evenings male reporters worked in their undershirts. Before I sat down at my typewriter at home I would pour water over my clothes, and when they dried I would dampen them again.

Topekans went to the hilltops to sleep. Cots and pallets were moved to backyards. Modesty and reserve were forgotten in the rush to the great open breathing spaces. After all, modesty and reserve are man-made virtues and would naturally be the first to go when a catastrophe of nature sends the human race back to the primitive. Outdoors, the nights were cool. Before morning children would wake with the strange plea, "Mamma, I'm cold," and mother would get up to spread covers on the family. People arose from their beds and said good morning to neighbors who had slept only a few feet away, then all went inside to put on a few clothes—as few as possible.

At first we spoke of the weather as a hot spell, but when it continued we dug in as for a siege. We were lucky. Our house had a wide front porch that wrapped itself around two sides. The children loved it. It was a great place to play and before the summer was over it became a good place to sleep. We moved our beds to the porch, bedsteads and all, and slept in view of any passersby for the rest of the summer. Willard was often away through the week by now, but the children and I slept there every night. My cousin Genevieve came from Colorado to visit us—she was about the same age as our son—and we worried about her, never having been in Kansas before and unused to hot weather. I worried about what she might think about sleeping on public display. But she did not complain and stayed her visit out.

For our vacation we drove to Colorado in a 1926 Chevy, the car windows open to the searing wind, the heat from the road making the bottom of the car too hot for our feet. We pushed on toward western Kansas and, we hoped, cooler nights.

A friend we stopped to visit proudly showed us a little tree he had tended and watered and kept alive. It was a tree that would not have got a second look anywhere else, but there it stood, green and surviving, a tiny monument to care and perseverance.

For the first night we stayed at the forerunner of the motel, but a very distant kin. It was a place to sleep merely, one from which to rise and go forth on the morrow. It had an outdoor toilet and a shower of tap water nearby, but who would want hot water anyway? It offered us all we needed for only two dollars.

The next day was Colorado, with my parents coming out to meet us as we drove up and a good dinner waiting. It was heavenly to be cool, to need quilts at night and a jacket for the evenings. The children loved the trip to the mountains. When Brother got a whiff of pine he ran in to say the mountains smelled just like cough syrup.

A pleasant aspect of a vacation is one's comparative disregard of the clock and calendar. Daylight starts another day and dark ends it, and it doesn't much matter whether it is Tuesday or Thursday. One evening I sat up to read after the rest were asleep. I read and read until it seemed that it must be nearly midnight. Thinking that in a very few hours my father would be rattling the ashes in the range, I undressed for bed and, as I put out the light, glanced at the clock. It was almost half past eight.

Sitting idly on the rocks and watching the creek go by, we thought it was a good place in which to stay forever. There were no telephones to shatter a bright reverie, no salesmen to stop at the door, and no young men to ask when our magazines expired. Towering cliffs and tall pines were our companions, and the only newspapers we saw were old ones in which we had packed our groceries. The world of busy people seemed far away and unimportant.

Deep in a pine forest, I learned the meaning of silence.

The pines, large and tall and old, were so close together that no branches grew on the lower part of their trunks. It was dark, cool, and sunless. Not a blade of grass or a weed grew anywhere, but the ground was covered with thick, soft moss, over which one walked with no more sound than is made by the moccasin of an Indian.

We sat on the moss eating snow from the deep bank which had survived in dark coolness. Around us was no sound of any other living thing, not even the soughing of wind through the pines. The Kansas drought was forgotten.

Chapter 32: Personalities

*W*e enjoyed town life and soon became a part of it. We played bridge, square danced with Preston and Anna Hale, friends from home who turned up in Topeka, and continued to subscribe to magazines to help deserving young men. We went often to see the Owls, Topeka's baseball team.

Our social center in summer was Baughman's ice cream plant in a bend of the Shunganunga Creek, which meandered through town on its way to the river and overflowed its banks after each heavy rain. I would occasionally take the children on an "adventure" when Willard was too busy to be distracted from work he brought home. I soon discovered that an early morning hike to the Shunganunga to cook bacon and eggs over a campfire, which stirred my pulse with a measure of thrill and excitement, was faint in comparison with the tremendous to-do it gave the children.

Loaded with skillets and provisions, we set forth in the early morning across the sleeping Washburn College campus, past small suburban homes where farmers were driving in cows to milk and where chickens ventured forth to try the new day. On to the banks of the creek, where with a sigh I sat down a heavy thermos jug and prepared to rest. But the lure of adventure urged the younger members of our party on to new fields. Just around that bend was the "swellest place," really it wasn't far, just across the cornfield, and around that meadow, then through the fence and along the creek a ways. Not a bit far was such a grand place.

It seemed to me that the place where we were was just as good as any, but, pressed by the restlessness of youth, I weakly allowed myself to be persuaded to take up my burdens again. The next time I certainly wouldn't bring a heavy jug. I decided that much.

The promised land seemed much like the place we had been—a bend in the creek. Perhaps the Shunganunga was a bit wider at that point and the banks a bit higher, but there were the same muddy, sluggish waters and the same sprawling vegetation. To young eyes filled with excitement, however, it was a wonderful stream, teeming with surprises, and the thin woods on its banks as mysteriously inviting as the deep jungles of the Amazon. The frogs, tadpoles, and minnows, the grasshoppers and buzzing life were as marvelous as strange creatures of an unknown world. And how we ate! Everything we had brought—and the children clamored for more.

Returning home, we stopped a few minutes to talk to a man plowing. Recalling the happy hours I had spent walking behind my father in the furrow, I asked if we might follow him; I didn't want the children to miss a pleasant farm experience. Dorothy Anne, then six, looked at me with a mixture of pity and scorn, and in a voice which struggled to be patient with the foibles of old age, said, "Plowing! What is there fun about *plowing*?"

Dorothy Anne always had a mind of her own. At age seven she asked, "When can I have a skirt, Mother?" When I reminded her that she already had skirts, she became impatient with my lack of understanding. "But they *button* on. I want a skirt that's *tight* around my waist." That took me back to a time when, at about her age, I asked my mother for a skirt and how elated, how right I felt when that blue and white cotton flapped around my skinny legs. It was no matter that my blouse would not stay tucked in when I played Blackman.

I remember, too, the waves of *déjà vu* when I was told that my great-granddaughter, April, at six years of age wanted a skirt. The badge of womanhood is, I gather, not long hair or long dresses, not high heels or silk stockings, not even lipstick, but a skirt. A skirt presupposes a slender waist and curving hips. Curving hips being feminine, skirts are feminine. Some instinct moves a small girl to want a skirt, a separate skirt, one tight around the waist.

It was still the Depression, but it wore a different face from the one we knew on the farm. Men came to the house peddling small articles. One selling needles and pins fitted me with the best thimble I ever had, not too tight, but tight enough to stay on; not too loose, but loose enough not to bind. He confided that his rheumatism was getting worse and that he couldn't get to sleep at night after tramping over hard pavement all day. He admitted that ever since that rainy season while prospecting up in Feather Canyon his rheumatism had been pretty bad.

So he had been a prospector. That explained the look of perennial hope on his face. With little encouragement he began telling about the Graham brothers, who were hard up and owed everybody at the camp. They finally struck gold and went around town paying off their debts in currency. They owed almost ten thousand dollars (which shows what good borrowers they were).

"I never made much money myself," he apologized. "When I got a little ahead, I always set out to look for another claim."

I felt there was no justice in the fact that a man who had "driven shafts" and built "slopes," a man who had wandered solitary amid the grandeur of mountain peaks, whose feet had tramped the soft soil of pine forests, a man who had searched for hidden treasure should tread city streets selling needles and pins.

Then there was the man who came to sharpen knives and scissors. He set up his grindstone in the yard and, before he left, every knife and pair of scissors was sharp. Jolly and laughing, he brought pleasure to our house, returning once or twice a year. We missed him when he didn't show up one year and wondered if he had family to return to.

But the one I can never forget, if his story was true, tottered up to the door, small and feeble, to hand in a card asking for help. It stated that he was deaf and afflicted with tuberculosis.

Consumed with shame and pity, I could not look into his eyes. They were the humble, appealing eyes of an animal caught in a trap, without pride or reservation, pleading for help. What must a human soul have suffered to reach such a state? I wrote on his slate that I would phone to see what could be done for him. But he handed me another card saying the local Provident Association could not help because he wasn't a resident and that the transient camp could not keep him because of his tuberculosis. They would pay his way to the state where he came from, but a doctor there had told him he would die unless he got to Arizona, and he wanted a little help to "get over the pass."

Why does he want to live, I wondered, as I handed him my pittance. His scribbled response said, "Thank you. So many people do not understand."

Each month my husband would cash his paycheck and go about sharing the wealth with the landlord, utility companies, and grocer, with whom we had our only charge account. When he paid that bill, he brought home as lagniappe a sack of candy. We did not open a bank account for several years.

This was also a time when young women came to the city to look for work. The YWCA offered them low-priced lodging, recreation, new friends, and help in finding a job. Some were enabled to send money back to their families. Now and then a father came in person to ask his daughter for a few dollars. I know because several of these girls lived with us as a member of the family, helped with the work, and became our friends.

One, a Swedish schoolteacher, at the close of the school year stored her car for the summer and came to the big city. A nice young man, a farmer who was later elected to the State

Legislature, came to visit her a few times and we listened for wedding bells. Instead she left for Denver. She seemed to have a deep-seated dread of living in the country. A real treasure, she not only did the cooking but planned the menus. Her meals were always full of delicious surprises, such as a fresh pie for which she climbed a tree in the backyard and picked the cherries. Here we were, refugees from the Depression, our combined salaries a little less than a hundred dollars a month, enjoying the luxury of a superb cook, housekeeper, and baby-sitter—for five dollars a week.

Another of our girls was deep, quiet, and smoldering, with big gray eyes and a low, rich voice. She sang with a local dance band and could put a world of loneliness into "Red Sails in the Sunset." A member of the band would stop by for her early in the evening and she would return late that night. (I don't remember that we ever had keys made for the house and I don't remember hearing about crime. Perhaps, like us, nobody had anything worth robbing.) With the coming of war, better jobs were provided for girls and soon no one was available for housework.

My job occasionally took me out of town. When they occurred on weekends, these trips became family outings, often accompanied by the Austins. We once drove to Hiawatha, Kansas, to see the love of a man for his wife expressed in fine Italian carrara marble and granite from the eternal hills of Vermont. John M. Davis had erected this striking memorial in the cemetery to the sacred memory of his "dearly beloved wife, Sarah." It has been called one of the most unique memorials in America. As we came up to it, an old man with a long, gray beard, his left arm missing, walked slowly away and started getting into his car.

"That man looks like the statue on the memorial," observed Mr. Austin. "I'll bet it's Mr. Davis."

It was, and he was kind in answering my questions. At seventy-nine, Mr. Davis had keen blue eyes and a ruddy face. He had come to Kansas in 1879 and moved to Hiawatha in 1915. His wife died there on December 3, 1930, at the age of seventy.

The memorial is made up of six groups of figures of himself and his wife at different periods of their life. At one end they are seated together on a bench, looking as they did when married for ten years. In two other groups, they stand facing each other as they did on their eighteenth and fiftieth wedding anniversaries. In the latter his arm is missing for the first time. (I thought it impolite to ask what happened.) Mr. Davis said his wife was not well for some time before her death and had not been able to ride in a car, so they spent many hours together on the front porch. They are shown sitting there in white marble, drawn to each other by deep sympathy and affection. By the side of this group is a figure of Mr. Davis sitting alone beside an empty chair, while the last group shows him with bowed head; beside him is the figure of his wife as an angel.

"They measure you closer than for a suit of clothes," said Mr. Davis, explaining how the figures were made. The sculptor made life-sized figures of clay, of which he sent photographs to Mr. Davis for criticism. At last the completed statuary was shipped to Hiawatha. We learned that Mr. Davis came every Sunday afternoon to the memorial and often, after a rain or storm, he came to clean and wash the monument.

"I'm not proud of it," he told us, "just thankful that I could do it. It hasn't been pleasant for me, for every time I come out here I have to go back without her."

"It must have been quite expensive," I suggested.

"So they say," he replied. "We don't get things like that for a song and sing it ourselves."

The body of Mrs. Davis lies beneath the polished granite floor of the memorial with a space for his own beside it. They had no children. Mr. Davis lived alone in the house they occupied for fifteen years; he said he often dreamed of the woman he loved. And looking at her beautiful face immortalized in purest stone, one does not wonder that her love filled his life completely or that he poured out his love for her in a glorious sonnet written in marble. It is the Taj Mahal of Kansas.

That last sentence makes me sound like one of the Kansas "boosters" who so abounded during the Depression, such as those who sponsored the dinner of the Kansas Co-Operative League, at which all the food served was grown in Kansas. The occasion was to prove that our state could live very comfortably, thank you, on what she produced within her own boundaries. There was a meat loaf made from beef that undoubtedly once roamed the Kansas prairies, potatoes from the Kaw Valley, salt from Reno, and beans from Wamego, among other things.

"Where was the coffee grown?" I teased Charley Moore, president of the organization.

"In Coffey County," he solemnly answered.

If the League had been a little more loyal to Kansas, they would have served an invigorating beverage which was brewed, I understand, in the southeastern part of the state, but the teetotaling boosters didn't lean over backwards in their partisanship and boosterism. Kansas, after all, had been legally dry since 1880, and the repeal of Prohibition was still some time away.

Bernarr Macfadden, noted publisher of *Physical Culture*, *Liberty*, and *True Story* magazines, was one of the interesting personalities of the day I was assigned to interview. He was the kind of person the press likes—spectacular and unpredictable. His well-shaped head was topped by a thick mass of graying black hair, his lined face gave the appearance of strength, and his keen blue-gray eyes smoldered and flashed as he talked.

Born in a little town in the Missouri Ozarks, he was orphaned early in life and, as a lonely child of eight or ten, was "adopted out" and had to look to strangers for care and affection. He didn't find a great deal of either.

Hard work was about all he found. He remembered sharply the bitter humiliation that he suffered when someone inquired who he was and was answered carelessly, "Oh, that's just the boy the Smiths adopted." That smarting hurt. Not to have a name of his own was the deepest wound his childish pride could suffer, and perhaps it stirred in his bruised young heart the ambition to make his name something more.

At one time he was a hired man on a farm at McCune, Kansas. He worked for the sum of ten dollars a month and when his employer dissented to his modest suggestion that he thought he was worth fifteen, he left. That has been one of the secrets of the Macfadden success—he knew when to quit a hopeless job and when to persevere in a discouraging one.

His *Physical Culture* magazine—in addition to being the beloved vehicle of his ambition (for he had a magnificent physique)—was incidentally the means of starting *True Story* magazine, which made him a great deal more money than *Physical Culture*. Many wrote to him in those early days, pouring out their stories, intimate, personal, often tragic tales of tangled lives, of mistakes and misunderstandings, of wrecked lives or eventual happiness.

He did not, as was thought at the time, live on an exclusive diet of cracked wheat, but he did sleep on the floor. And he gave me a recipe for getting through a hot night. At the hotel where he had stayed the night before, he pulled a few covers down to the floors, set a fan nearby, and hung up a few wet bath towels for the fan to blow through. Then he went to bed, having first put a couple more wet towels over the sheet to sleep on. "Do this," he said, "and you'll never know the night is hot."

Many great and famous trekked to Topeka that summer to interview our presidential candidate, Alf Landon, but none was more pleasant than "that boy the Smiths adopted."

I am reminded of the Orphans' Home in Atchison, where I visited that summer with Grace Axton, its superintendent. She confirmed a statement I had heard many times before: that it is little girls with blue eyes and golden curls whom people want when adopting a baby. "There are more than twice as many boys as girls at the home," Mrs. Axton told me, "adorable little boys, too." While little girls are no longer cast away to perish, a son is nevertheless greatly hoped for to carry on the family name and fortune. A daughter might manage the fortune, but she cannot perpetuate the family name, though why in the world some families want it perpetuated, I do not know.

So if a family cannot have a son of their own flesh and blood to bear their name rightfully and bequeath it to sons of their own, they would prefer to have none, and instead choose a lovely daughter to comfort them, for daughters change their names anyway and are soon lost in the family identity. At any rate, the truth is that parents prefer a boy when it is their own and a girl when it is adopted. Another golden age will be here when supply and demand can be made to work in human needs.

One who wasn't at all what I had expected him to be was H. L. Mencken. His ruddy face and penetrating blue eyes gave an impression of openness and frank curiosity. He was friendly, what an old neighbor used to call "chatty," with no pose of the intelligentsia about him. Although a Democrat, Mencken supported Landon, expecting to be with him during much of the campaign. "If Landon's a Pennsylvania Dutchman," he said, "brought up in the Middle West, he is well nigh perfect. He's no orator, but thank God for that. We've had too much oratory. Franklin Roosevelt knows more than he does, but more of what he knows isn't true."

After a few minutes' talk with Mencken, you felt as if you had known him a long time. I was somewhat chagrined when he laughingly mentioned what Mr. Runyon thought about something or other. "You mean Damon Runyon?" I asked. "Is he here?" I learned that I had been sitting next to Mr. and Mrs. Damon Runyon all evening. They were representing the *New York American*. Some of my favorite columns were written that week.

Chapter 33: The Settling of Dusk

"*Z*ula, be careful now."

I cherished that first name, believing for years that it came from a romantic novel my mother or aunts had read. In my youth I patterned my deportment in ways I deemed suitable for a glamorous heroine transported by fate to a rural environment in the Middle West. It was not until 1935, my fortieth year, that I learned its source. A reader questioned its origin, and with no small chagrin I responded that I would have to ask my mother. Her letter was revealing.

It seems that since their home had been blessed with a girl, my parents were confident the impending offspring would be a boy. They had fine names awaiting their son and heir, but none for a second daughter. When the delivering doctor asked my name, my nonplussed parents could think of nothing feminine, so the doctor, probably anxious to smooth over a bad situation, asked if they wouldn't like to name me after his daughter, Zula. A romantic maiden aunt present thought that would be "just sweet—and so different!" and, my parents raising no dissenting voice, it was done.

After a considerable absence, I returned to my childhood home in Missouri for a family reunion at a time when most of the ninety-four descendants of my maternal grandparents were able to attend. The startling discovery was that everything had shrunk. Places separated in memory by long stretches of dreamy distance had moved much closer together. The hill I remembered as a splendid long sweep from back door to fence had collapsed to a mere rise and snuggled against the old house for companionship. Only the mulberry trees were familiar, looking older and gaunt, as did my kinfolk.

I walked the still familiar paths over which I used to drive the cows at night, lingering at the pond, now dry and empty, where I paused to listen to the croaking of the frogs. I hated to acknowledge how hopeless it is to recapture the glamour of childhood. Decades are decades, and the little girl who drove cows over narrow paths skirting mossy rocks and gnarled trees was only somebody whom I had known a long time ago, one toward whom I felt warm affection, whose memory was tender and amusing, but who was no longer on my Christmas card list. Startled by the settling of dusk, I rushed over the last lap and arrived at the house breathless, hoping my absence had not been noticed.

Visiting the family cemetery the next day, I realized that somewhere in the earth rest the ashes of all those whose lives had united to form my own—savages, peasants, warriors, the ruthless, the gentle, the ignorant, the wise, the cowardly, the courageous—links welded together slowly, generation by generation, to form this highly valued and greatly prized bit of flesh and blood we call our self. Their ashes may rest in the earth, but they are not dead. That spark of life kindled in them burned for a while and lighted fires in other limbs. Today our vanity tells us we are the link for which all other links in the great chain of being were made. But tomorrow the young life in which we have lighted the fire will become supreme and, when we have joined the silent forms whose fire has been extinguished, our children will live and our children's children, and on and on into the future, as dim, unpredictable, and endless as the past.

In the cool, green silence of the cemetery, thinking of that long chain, I knew that I too shall rest in the earth and that life will go on much the same as before. There our little affairs become less important.

I was recalled from my reveries by Willard, who wondered where I had gone and had come to find me. After the last meal the next day, kissing distant cousins and promising to keep in closer touch, we left, taking a long route home to Topeka, meandering into the cool of the Ozarks. Refreshed, we started our journey again and, reaching Topeka, settled into our daily routines once more.

Our farm in Chase County had been rented to a neighbor and we returned to it frequently. The first time we went home, Dorothy Anne informed a neighbor, "We're going back to Kansas!" I must admit it did seem to be a different state as our car headed toward our beloved Flint Hills.

That glorious spring evening I walked out into the yard and saw through the honey locusts the great disk of the moon, which made a silver lake of the tin roof of the cowshed.

No sound could be heard except the faint rustle of the cottonwood and the far-off chirping of some lone insect.

I saw the lilac hedge with its swoon-inducing fragrance, the dark shadows of the hills, and, winding before me, the worn path to the house. How many times and with what feelings had it been traveled. One year, five years, ten, and a person stands in the same place and looks at the same moon through the same trees.

How alike everything is and how different, a part of you left everywhere you have been.

Afterword

The Chief End of Life

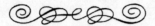

Old age can be tragic: weakened physical and mental powers, children married and gone, friends departed, lack of money for needs and comforts, the feeling of no longer being a useful part of society. There is small comfort in this world for the helpless, bewildered, and lonely whose generation has passed on. The world becomes unfamiliar. Death is the final and perhaps welcome step of dissolution.

Now in my ninth decade, I no longer dread becoming old. Nor do I fear becoming childish. Finding delight in the smallest and most inconsequential happenings, I have regained the wonder and joy of my youth. Old age when unhampered by want and worry is a lovely and satisfying time of life.

In quiet moments I find myself thinking about all that has been said about the chief aim of life. Some have thought it to be happiness, some service, and the Presbyterian catechism has it "to glorify God and serve Him forever." But I now rather think the chief end of life is understanding desire.

All my life I wanted things. The first was a doll with human hair, a wonderful creation that could talk and sleep. I mentioned it steadily in my prayers, for at the time God and Santa Claus were pretty much the same in my mind. (For that matter, I am still a little confused about the difference.) Also on that long list of childhood desires were a red dress, a big floppy straw hat, gloves instead of mittens, a little wagon, and later a bicycle.

College stimulated new desires. I aspired to a blue silk dress and a white coat. But my greatest longing was for a purple silk parasol. For years I grabbed the Montgomery Ward catalogue the minute the mailman left it in our box to see what they were asking for purple silk parasols. And for several now forgotten reasons I wanted red corduroy lounging pajamas. I knew there would never be time for lounging on the farm, but I yearned for them anyway. Then I discovered it gave more pleasure and didn't cost any more to wish for red velvet. So I changed my fancy and imagined a leisured elegance in red velvet pajamas.

Of the many things I have wanted, some I got but most I didn't. Looking back, I can see that they were not truly extravagances, and I could doubtless have caught a few old hens and sold them for enough to have bought a purple parasol. But I'm rather glad I didn't, for the memory of unfulfilled desires is brighter than that of those realized. The Grecian evening gown I wanted—and got—turned out to be disappointment, but the red lounging pajamas are still a delight and that white coat is a vision of loveliness.

I feel toward them as a man does toward an old sweetheart he didn't marry. The charm and mystery of his wife are pretty well worn off by daily life together. While he is without doubt fond of her, sometimes of an evening who knows but that he calls up the memory of his old love and clothes her with a beauty and disposition that would astonish her husband.

And so it is with those things I wanted most and never got. I did not see them tarnish, fade, rip, or grow dim with age.

About the Authors

*J*ula Bennington Greene was born in Hickory County, Missouri, in 1895. As a young farmer's wife in the Kansas Flint Hills, she began writing a column for the *Chase County Leader*. It was soon carried by more than a dozen regional newspapers. From 1933 until her death in 1988 she enjoyed what may be the longest tenure of any daily columnist in the history of American journalism, filing six columns a week for the *Topeka Daily Capital*, later renamed the *Topeka Capital-Journal*. In 1983, she published a selection of these columns as *Skimming the Cream* and was featured on the MacNeil/Lehrer NewsHour. Her many honors included "Outstanding Newswoman of the Year" from both the University of Kansas and Kansas State University and a doctorate of humane letters from Washburn University. She was a charter member, board member, and president of the Topeka Civic Theatre, whose green room is still named the "Greene Room" in her honor. She died in 1988.

*E*ric McHenry is an assistant professor of English at Washburn University and the author of two books of poetry.

CPSIA information can be obtained at www.ICGtesting.com
Printed in the USA
LVOW08*1831081113

360563LV00002B/21/P